Tinpot and Proud
(Stagni Ollam et Superbus)

An account of some of those who have
contributed to the foundation of
Crawley Town FC, from its conception
in 1890 through to the present day.
Plus, a collection of "Thoughts of a Lifelong Fan"
as published in the Crawley Observer, covering
the 2021/2022 and 2022/2023 EFL 2 seasons.

Steve Leake

Cover by Matthew Leake

With many thanks to all who contributed to this book,
either through their memories or by jogging mine,
Including; Dannie Bulman, Lewis Young, Sarah Markham,
the family of Eric Strange and the Church of St. John, Crawley.

Thanks also to those who provided photographs,
Including; Mark Dunford (Crawley Observer),
Mick Fox, and Nadine Hygate through her "Wayfarer
Denman's Crawley Revisited" publication.

Special thanks to the town of Crawley, of which I am so proud,
and all those associated with Crawley Town FC.

"Grudges are for those who insist that they are owed something; forgiveness, however, is for those who are substantial enough to move on."

— **Criss Jami**

CONTENTS

Preface

I started writing this book back in 2021, when Crawley Town were owned by Ziya Eren, and John Yems was our manager. Since then, we have been bought by WAGMI and a lot of troubled water has flown under the bridge which has taken us from our Turkish owners to the ownership by our American friends.

I thought of putting the word, friends, in speech marks, to indicate how some of our fanbase think of them, but I decided not to as Preston Johnson, in particular, has become a friend of mine, and indeed of my whole family.

Tinpot and Proud will take you from the moment a 12-year-old Crawley boy learnt how to kick a football for the first time through 133 years of the development of the club we support. It features many of the people who have contributed to the club in so many ways and also, through my "Thoughts of a lifelong fan" covers what has probably been two of the most turbulent years in our history.

WARNING: The thoughts expressed in the second part of TINPOT AND PROUD are mine. I'm not sure if anyone thinks the same way as I do, but then that is what makes Football such a wonderfully emotional game, way of life or however you think of it in your lives. The thoughts were written, mostly on Sundays, and the dates that precede them are the issue dates of the Crawley Observer they appeared in. You will probably see that my mood still fluctuates according to results and I guess that is something we all have in common.

There will inevitably be other people that, you the fans would have included, but I need to have something to write about before I go up to the stadium in the sky, don't I?

I hope you enjoy the read, and if you're not in it, once again apologies from me, but, hopefully, when I write the next book "Champions League, here we come" I will have covered as many of you as possible.

Seriously, if you can think of a title for my next book please get in touch. My address, on every other Saturday during the football season, is "Sergio Corner, The Winfield Terrace, Broadfield Stadium, Winfield Way, Broadfield, Crawley RH11 9RX".

Steve Leake "A Lifelong fan"

Part One

Chapter One

The Founding Fathers

In the 19th century Crawley was just a small rural town in the north of the county of Sussex. The population was around 4000, which, to put it into perspective, is approximately the same size as the two smallest neighbourhoods, West Green and Northgate, that now exist and just under a third of the size of its largest, Pound Hill. Forty-nine years prior to the first friendly game played by Crawley FC, the main London to Brighton railway was opened in 1841, the area being served by a brand-new station called East Crawley, later to become Three Bridges. Seven years later the Three Bridges to Horsham line was opened and a Crawley station was built next to the level crossing between the High Street and Brighton Road. The Victorian New Town of Crawley was taking shape.

Two years earlier than the Brighton line opening, John Barrett-Lennard was born the fifth son of Sir Thomas Barrett-Lennard and Mary Shedden in 1839. During John's childhood the family would spend most of their summers in and around Brighton when it first became fashionable after changing its name from the longer Brighthelmstone at the beginning of the 19th century. In adult life he had a short military career as a lieutenant in the Royal Engineers, but resigned his commission and took up the cloth, finally arriving in Crawley as the Rector of St John the Baptist, after several junior posts in the Church of England in Shropshire and London, in 1876. He arrived in Crawley with his wife Isabella, the daughter of Sir John Lambton Loraine, and their three children, Constance, Emily Isabella and Herbert

Loraine and in 1889 he was introducing some of the young lads in the town to the joys of the beautiful game, when he came across a 12-year-old, William Denman, who had never seen a football before, let alone kicked one. Willy, as he was known then, was just watching the other boys when suddenly the Rector asked him why he was not playing. He explained that he didn't know how to as he had never seen a football before, to which the Rector placed a ball six yards in front of him and said "Now, run and kick hard".

This was Willy's response as told to Nadine Hygate in later years "I did so, and oh my relief, when I found that my foot was still attached to my leg"

And so commenced his second great passion in life, after cricket, and when Crawley FC was formed in 1890 to play friendlies, he became a player member at the ripe old age of 12.

By the age of 14, William, Bill, Willy Denman was the secretary of Crawley FC and just two years later he added the position of Cricket club secretary to his areas of responsibility, whilst also playing for both clubs. This wasn't the extent of his sporting prowess however, as he was also an active member of Crawley Harriers Athletic Club and Crawley Cycling Club. Having completed his formal education at the ripe old age of 12, he earned his keep by delivering milk for the neighbouring farmer, Mr. Tyler, and when he reached 16 he worked as a postman, working long hours delivering and receiving mail from the London to Brighton horse drawn night coaches at their stopping points, The Black Swan, Pease Pottage and Chequers at Horley. This obviously did not seem enough for the young man, as just one year later he started writing for local papers and magazines under the pseudonym "Wayfarer". I think this is what captured my imagination as I could see so many similarities in our lives, the love of sport, the love of Crawley and the love of history and writing about it.

By 1902, he was still Club Secretary at the age of 25.

You will also, no doubt, notice some other familiar Crawley names included in the club directory, (see pictures). They not only played their part in our club, but also in the building of our town, through the first new town, brought about by the railways, right through to the New Town, brought about by Hitler's bombing of the capital during the Second World War. Back in 1903, Bill married Helen Fielder of West Street on the 15th of April. The ceremony took place on a Wednesday as Bill was involved three days later in playing left wing for Crawley FC in the final of the Mid-Sussex Football League Challenge Shield, which they won for the first time in their relatively short history. Perhaps current Crawley Town supporters should revert to the custom of wearing red geraniums in their buttonholes as a sign of their allegiance. The club's pitch was Mr. Stone's field on Malthouse farm, between Brighton Road and Malthouse Road, whilst the headquarters were at the nearby Railway Inn, by the old Crawley station and level crossing.

Obviously, a well-respected and loved man, as shown in this extract from the write up of Bill's and Helen's wedding.

"Mr. Denman is the secretary of the Crawley Football and Cricket Clubs, and there is probably not another person in the town who has worked so hard in this direction than he. His abilities on the field – no matter whether cricket or football – have gained him a good deal of popularity, which has been increased by his ably discharged secretarial duties."

The ceremony was conducted by Rector Herbert Barrett-Lennard, the son of the Rector who had introduced Bill to football in 1889. Herbert taking over from his father, who sadly died in 1898 at the relatively young age of 59.

All our families are governed by twists of fate, coincidences, or divine intervention, depending on your beliefs. None more so than whether people survive, or not, the cruelty of war.

Bill Denman was 37 when the Great War broke out because of family squabbles in the Balkans. They should have been more like the Denman's, for in 1906 Bill and Helen took on Mabel, the eleven-year-old daughter of his eldest brother Tom and his wife Emily, who died giving birth to their son Albert who also died.

Her death, according to Nadine Hygate, was "shortly followed by Tom, who was heartbroken by his wife's death".

Bill's sister, Elsie Mitchell, took on the other two orphaned children, Victoria and Edgar, showing what true family unity is all about.

Further tragedy was to strike Bill's family before the war, when, in 1912 his father, John "Broomdasher" Denman died, after a long illness, at the relatively young age of 69. I say relatively as I am over that age myself and have absolutely no intention of entering the final clearing yet. Broomdasher refers to John's trade as a maker of brooms, a thriving local industry at the time, which is where the Three Bridges Street gets its name.

At the outbreak of war, Bill enlisted in the 1st Essex Regiment, going to France and became a Corporal, working in the cookhouse section. One day while in camp, his two slightly younger nephews, James and William Johnson, sons of another of his sisters, Annie, were passing through on their way to the front. They managed to meet up, and all three had a night out on the town, before the two younger boys continued on their way to Ypres. That was the last time Bill saw them, as on the 27th of February 1915 James was killed in action and William was badly injured and sent back to "blighty" to recover. James was just 23 years old and had joined the East Yorks, as a 17-year-old, six years previously. His body was never found but he is commemorated on Panel 21 of the Menin Gate and on the Crawley Memorial Garden Gates.

Just over a year later, his father John Johnson, a stockman at Belle Vue farm on the Tilgate estate took his own life with his shot gun, because of the death of James, the injury to William and the impending enlistment of a third son John (Jack). Shortly before his suicide he was heard to say, "This is the last blow, we have sacrificed two, and that ought to be enough." He left his wife and five children still at home at Belle Vue farm, which is situated between the M23 and the new housing development by Parish Lane in Pease Pottage, but now known as Hardriding cottages.

4

As sure as night follows day. William Johnson was also killed in action on the 3rd of May 1917, and just like his brother, his body was also never found. He too, is also commemorated on the Memeorial Garden Gates and the memorial at Arras.

Lest we forget. (Credit to Nadine Hygate "Wayfarer Denman's Crawley Revisited" and Renny Richardson "All the bright company of heaven"

After the Great War, which killed over twenty million people, roughly half of which were military personnel and just over half of them from the allied forces, my Granddad, Albert Edward Pinfold, who had served in the RAMC, and had witnessed the famous Christmas football match between opposing combatants, like Bill had experienced the devastation of trench warfare and the absolute horror of gas attacks. The effect of the gas on Bill was to give him severe breathing difficulties and the rotting of all his teeth. They were removed without the use of anaesthetic by an army medic wielding a pair of pliers, and, after a period of convalescence, he was returned to his unit until he was demobbed. Bill returned home to the devastating news about his brother-in-law and nephews and dedicated his life to his local community in more ways than one, whereas my granddad returned home, to make sure, indirectly, that my time would come.

Crawley for Bill must have seemed like paradise compared to Ypres and the Somme, but like today the country was quickly thrown into a pandemic situation with the onset of Spanish Flu, which claimed 228,000 lives in the United Kingdom alone.

In between the Great War and its sequel, which allowed it to be called the First World War, Bill was a very busy man. He survived both war and pestilence and at home, in Station Road, when it housed the police station and several Victorian houses, the family grew to five again with the birth of James Fielder, his youngest son. Bill was elected for Ifield Parish on the Horsham Rural Council, despite living in Crawley, and, along with some friends, was responsible for the setting up of the Crawley Labour

5

party. Party politics at the time did not feature in local councils and thus Bill was able to represent his electorate's best interests.

He was also involved with St John's Church and served on numerous committees, including the Education Committee of West Sussex County Council. All this, plus his sporting interests and writing on local matters, inevitably meant that in 1928 he hung up his boots for Crawley FC at the age of 51, which makes Dannie Bulman seem like a youngster.

In 1932, he became the first Crawley born man to be made a justice of the Peace and was, at the time, chairman of Crawley FC. This may not have happened if a bizarre incident involving his duties had not concluded so benignly. Whilst raising the flag on the church tower, he had to climb on the parapet of the tower. One day he was late returning home for his lunch, so his wife Helen went to the front gate of their Station Road home to see if she could see him. She must have been astonished to see him clinging to the flag's rope, over the side of the tower. He had been hanging there for about half an hour and was eventually rescued by their neighbours, the local police. A bad case of wind, the meteorological kind, being the cause of the incident.

Crawley FC folded in 1935, only to be resurrected three years later. In fact, the new Crawley FC (still not Town) was an amalgamation of interested parties from three clubs but with most of the officers coming from the old Crawley FC. The two other clubs were Crawley Athletic and Crawley Rangers.

On 31st of December 1937, Bill retired, after 43 years of service, from the postal service. He had worked under six postmasters and had worked his way up to the post (excuse the pun) of head postman by 1924, the position from which he retired. According to Nadine Hygate's account in "Crawley revisited" he was still chairman of both the football and cricket clubs and was also heavily involved in numerous local concerns including the Rifle club, the British Legion, Crawley Harriers, Crawley Gardeners, Crawley and Ifield Old Boys and was also one of the managers of the council schools.

With all this public service, alongside his writing for about six local papers, he could hardly have had any spare time, even in retirement. Sports was reported under the pseudonym Onlooker, while his diary reports on all things Crawley, appeared under the Wayfarer banner, which, contrary to my earlier belief, he did not take up until after the First World War, inheriting that title from Caleb Thornton. He did, however, write to a variety of papers under his own name on matters of local interest.

As with most families there were also times of sadness and poor health and in the late 30s, Helen, his wife, became very ill, culminating in an operation for cancer in Crawley Cottage Hospital. She convalesced with friends in Brighton, at which time Bill contracted Whooping Cough, no doubt made worse by his mustard gas affected lungs and the smoky atmosphere in all the committees he was in.

Bill, having served in the war to end all wars, must have been devastated when World War 2 started in 1939, not just because it put a temporary halt to football for the new Crawley FC, but also because two of his sons enlisted to face the same enemy that he had, just 25 years earlier. Helen, from 1942 to 1944, endured a long fight against cancer with Bill spending every night looking after her until she eventually passed away in May 1944. He never got over losing his wife but kept on in public service even though his own health was deteriorating. In April 1945, he stood as an independent, despite being a staunch Labour man, for the local council, as he didn't believe in party politics at local level. He won with a large majority, and was elected Chair, in his absence, at the council's first meeting.

On the 8th of May 1945, Victory in Europe was achieved, and Bill decorated his house with bunting from George VI's coronation in 1937. Just one day later, he passed away from lung cancer, and the bunting was taken down.

The Rector, at his funeral, concluded his talk with "For Mr. Denman we may say "Thank God. May this country go on producing men who are prepared to give themselves to the public service as he did". On the day of the funeral Crawley came to a halt, as he was laid to rest with Helen in St John's churchyard.

"No working man in Sussex could have had a finer life than I have had – full of sport and interesting events, and everyone has been really good to me" W J Denman 31st December 1937

By getting this far, you will know that Bill Denman was not the only man responsible for the development of both our town and our football club. I have already introduced you to Rev Johm Barrett-Lennard, the rector who introduced Bill to the beautiful game, but I feel the need to elaborate a little about him, as he too seemed an incredible force of nature. He came to Crawley in 1876, the youngest son of a Baron, along with his wife and three children, one of which, Herbert, would take over at St John's upon his father's death. He was described as an exponent of "muscular Christianity" which displayed itself in his work with the youth of Crawley, teaching them how to box and play football. The church, before he came, had deteriorated as far as the fabric was concerned but he, as an "upright Victorian gentleman", set about rectifying that and was seen as a key driver in the growth of the three villages, Three Bridges, Crawley and Ifield. He was also a keen carpenter, as can be seen from the rector's chair that he made and in other carvings within St. John's. A sign of how much he was thought of by his congregation is to be seen in the commemorative plaque and stained-glass window installed in the church.

The other person who also played a big part in the early years of Crawley FC was George Francis Hampton Banks, who, like his namesake Gordon, appears to have been a goalkeeper. Unlike the World cup winning Gordon, he was also Crawley's Chairman. Born in 1870, he was the son of the Rector of Worth, and thus was in a different social stratum to our Bill, but just twenty odd years later they were united through Crawley FC.

An architect/builder, he worked on the ongoing renovations at St Johns in 1911, under Rector Herbert Barret-Lennard. He was also married in 1911, but, like Bill, set off for war just three years later with the Sussex Regiment, holding the rank of Lieutenant.

In 1916, in the second month of the Battle of the Somme, George was injured, either at Delville Wood or Pozieres, but at least he lived to fight again and serve his community, unlike so many others.

On the first day of the battle, there were approximately 20.000 British fatalities, one death every 4.4 seconds including 37 sets of brothers, leading to the disbanding of "Old Pals" regiments because of the devastating affect it was having on communities back home. Away from Crawley FC, Captain Wilfrid Nevill, aged 21, of the East Surrey regiment, signaled his men to advance by kicking one of two footballs towards the enemy lines. It is thought he knew that the British Artillery bombardment had had little or no effect on the German trenches, and that the football would keep his men's minds off the carnage that was about to happen. The East Surreys did make their target for the attack, but Captain Nevill was shot in the head and died from his wounds. The two balls, with their inscriptions, "The Great European Cup" and "East Surrey versus Bavarians" were rescued from the battlefield

George Banks continued as Chairman of Crawley FC up until 1938, although it must be noted that for the last three years the club did not play any matches as negotiations took place to replace the three Crawley clubs, Rangers, Athletic and "FC" with just the one organisation. The fact that the new club inherited the name and history of Crawley FC, rather than that of the other two, implies, I think, that most of the officials for the new club were old "FC" committee members. So, it was in 1938 Norman Longley took over the reins as chairman of the "new" club and George became President.

One year later the club had to move grounds because of the development of the old Malthouse Farm site, probably by Longley Builders, and they were due to play at a site donated by local farmer and purveyor of fine sausages, Mr. Yetman. As noted in Noli Semper Cedere this was where Sunny Mead is now, in West Green. At the AGM for the Club, in July 1939, there was great excitement about the move, which, thanks to the sequel to the Great War, did not happen properly until the 1945-46 season.

The Sussex and Surrey Courier July 15th, 1939 featured this comment about GFH Banks, under the sub-title election of officers "Mr. Banks was re-elected president on the motion of the chairman, who said "Crawley FC would not really be "Crawley" unless Mr. Banks was at the helm of it" (Applause). Mr. Banks accepted office." Note the formality of the language which rather underplayed the affection for the man. He continued in the role of President through to the early 50s, marking over 60 years association with Crawley FC, and sadly died on October 17th, 1960, at 90 years of age, two days after the team had been beaten by local rivals, Horsham, by one goal to nil in front of over 1000 spectators at Town Meadow. May I suggest, as my good friend Mick Fox did in the Mansfield Town programme, that if you are in love with Crawley Town as much as I am, that the next time you are in town you visit St John the Baptist church, and have a look for yourselves at the resting places of WJ Denman, Rev John Barrett-Lennard and George Francis Hampton Banks. Think about the contributions these people made to our club and our town and, whatever level of spirituality you are happy with, offer up a word or two of thanks to these people of vision. If the church is open, have a look at the Barrett-Lennard memorial stain glass window, then take a walk down to the Memorial gardens and spend some time thinking about the Johnson brothers and others who gave their lives for their country, and are now commemorated on the gates where friendlies would have been played back in 1890. Norman Longley, knighted in 1966, played a big part in the building of the second New Town, the first coming in the previous century with the arrival of the railways, and that is probably why by the early 50s he had handed over the reins to George Hide, who along with manager Fred Cunnell, was responsible for the next legend, Stan Markham, signing for Crawley FC.

Bill Denman, John Barrett-Lennard and George Banks all played significant roles in the birth and infancy of the club we now call Crawley Town. For me, being a true Red Devil, I am grateful for the numerous chains of events that must have happened for John to become a vicar and for him to introduce Bill to the beautiful game. That is without the introduction of George as goalkeeper, chairman and president. Chains which were forged through the meeting of men and women, some upper class, some middle and some working class, but all whose roads led to a small village in North Sussex. Chains which could have been broken, like so many others were, by the ravages of war, but somehow remained intact and became a part of the Crawley FC machine. Likewise, I am thankful that my family chains also brought me to the town I love, when war brought my mum and dad together and luckily, they chose Crawley as the New Town they were to settle in. To think it could have been Stevenage makes me truly grateful, as without the move to Sussex my family simply would not exist as I know it. John, Bill and George were all key characters in our development, but none were able to claim the moniker of "Mr. Crawley Town". Not because they did not deserve such recognition, but simply because the club were yet to acquire the "Town" suffix.

Chapter Two

The New Town Years

Stan Markham was the first man to be recognised as "Mr. Crawley Town" but before we get to his status and influence within the club we need to look back at where his link in the chain was forged. On January 12th, 1926, Stanley was born in the London borough of Lambeth at St Thomas' Hospital. To put this into chronological perspective, just fourteen days later John Logie Baird presented the first live demonstration of television and Crawley, to Stan's family, was just a small town with a population of just under 6000, halfway between London and Brighton. Crawley, as far as football was concerned, featured three clubs, Rangers, Athletic and FC, with FC playing in the Mid Sussex league at Victoria Hall, Northgate, roughly where the Alms houses are now. One of four children, Stanley grew up in Lambeth where he attended the Laxton Street Junior School, and this is where his football "career" began with an astonishing amount of success as borne out by this anecdote he passed on to his family later in life.

"We won the lot. Everything that was open to junior schools in the area, we won it".

At the age of 11 he moved up to Chaucer Street Senior Boys School in Bermondsey where he made the position of goalkeeper his own and indeed, his prowess in between the sticks soon paid dividends with a final victory by two goals to one in the final of the Millwall Shield, over St Michael's of Dockhead in 1938. Success bred his love of the game, and he was fortunate to have played on the first floodlit public football pitch at Tabard Park, off Old Kent Road, just before the lights started going out all over Europe.

Being a retired teacher and a person who loves history, Tabard Park was built on the site of an old inn known back in the 14th century as the Tabard, and referred to by Chaucer as the starting point for pilgrims on route the shrine of Thomas à Becket in Canterbury. The Inn was later known as the Talbot, but that was demolished in the late 19th century and the area became notorious for slum housing until it was cleared in the late 1920s to make room for the ahead of its time, Tabard Park.

When Neville Chamberlain flew back from Munich on the 30th September 1938 promising peace in our time, Stanley Markham was just twelve and a half years old and no doubt looking forward to progressing in the game he loved. Just one year later, following the invasion of Poland by Germany, the future, not just for young Stanley, was put on hold.

Stan, like a lot of other London children, was evacuated to Devon, no doubt in an attempt to keep him safe from the Blitz. He was brought home to the capital just as the Germans shifted their effort to other cities, which was probably a stroke of luck for him, as Plymouth was targeted in the spring of 1941 and caused the deaths of 1,172 civilians and 4,448 injuries. Many London families brought their children home at this time, probably thinking that no place was safe and that it would be better to be together as families. At the ripe old age of 14 he left school and worked as a trainee mechanic for Sainsbury and when he reached the age of 18, he enlisted in the Grenadier Guards and served as a Fitters Mate in the Guards Armoured Division. Just six months into his military life he was in the thick of the action in Operation Market Garden. Between fifteen and seventeen thousand allied troops were to die in this operation, being under constant fire from the Germans as they ventured across Holland on a narrow two-lane road nicknamed "Hells Highway". However, despite heavy German resistance, the Allies captured the bridges across the Waal in Nijmegen on the 20th of September 1944, and an eighteen-and-a-half-year-old lived to fight another day.

When the lights came on again all over the world in 1945 Stan stayed in the army for another two years, stationed first in

Germany and then at Crickoweth in Welsh Wales. Whilst in the army he played in goal for his regiment and not only impressed his commanding officer, who stated that Stan's Military conduct was exemplary, displaying an enthusiastic personality who was keen, trustworthy and hardworking, but also managed to catch the eye of Tottenham Hotspur.

Upon leaving the army he was made an offer by Spurs on the 24th of May 1947, initially as an amateur player, but just three and a half months later he was awarded his first professional contract on the 5th of September.

Away from the football Stan was also a keen cricketer, and it was whilst he was playing cricket that he met his wife to be, Alma. Alma's and Stan's fathers were both police officers in the Metropolitan police and when Alma's father retired, he took over the running of the District Sports club for the Metropolitan Police, The Warren, in Hayes, Middlesex. Alma's family lived on site and she kept the score for a cricket game in which Stan was playing. I don't know whether he bowled a maiden over, but just a year later, in 1948, Stan and Alma were married in Riddlesdown, Purley.

Stan's signing for Tottenham Hotspur found him in illustrious company, with the likes of Alf (later to become the World Cup winning Sir Alf) Ramsey, Bill (36-years with Tottenham Hotspur as player and manager during which time they won eight major trophies including the League and Cup double in 1960/61) Nicholson and probably most significantly, Ted Ditchburn, the first-choice keeper, as squad members.

Ted, like Stan, played during the war, but only for Spurs when he was able to, depending on his RAF duties. He made his debut for Tottenham in a 1940 Wartime league match against Chelsea, but such were the vagaries of war that he was also able to guest for Aberdeen because he was stationed at nearby Lossiemouth. Being ahead of Stan in signing for Spurs meant that he was already the first choice between the sticks when Stan joined their ranks. In fact, he went on to play 452 times for the club, including an unbroken run of 247 matches between 1948 and 1954.

14

Nevertheless, Stan did not let this affect him, as he was happy being a permanent fixture in the squad and being paid for what he loved to do. He went on to make 105 appearances for Tottenham, one for the first team against Erith, forty-seven for the reserves and 57 for the A team. Unfortunately, in the year I moved to Crawley, 1952, he sustained a serious wrist injury, which, after an unsuccessful operation, brought an end to his professional career.

One match that did stand out in Stan's memory of his time at Spurs, was a London Challenge cup tie against Charlton Athletic at the Valley. He had played really well during the game, but with the score standing at one all the Valiants/Addicks were awarded a penalty in the dying seconds. The centre forward hit his shot hard and low to Stan's left but he pulled off a fine save which took the tie to a replay. Unfortunately, Spurs lost that game three one.

He signed for Wisbech Town of the Midland League for the 1952/53 season, travelling up from his two bed Chingford flat in London for training and games. A year later saw him sign for Canterbury City where he played for three seasons. Like a lot of Football clubs City have had their ups and downs over the years and the club that bears the name now only came into being in 2007. Consequently, playing records are hard to find for Stan's tenure at Brett's corner, but suffice it to say that, in his first season there, City won the Kent Senior Cup, against Tunbridge Wells, for the first and last time in their history.

After three seasons in Kent, Stan picked up a copy of the Sporting Record and responded to an advert for new players for Crawley FC to coincide with their joining of the Metropolitan League. We were still two years away from adding "Town" to our name but the move to Crawley was seen as an attractive proposition by Stan and Alma as it would allow them and their two children to move from their two-bed flat In Chingford to a three-bed house in Crawley with its own garden and surrounding countryside.

In the 1955-56 Season, Canterbury City finished 7th in the Kent County League First Division, and let in fewer goals than they scored, whereas Crawley FC finished second in the Sussex County League with 96 goals scored against 28 conceded and only four games lost. Whether it was the football or the lure of a decent house and garden, in what was being dubbed "The finest town in England", that attracted Stan and Alma is a matter of conjecture, but in May 1956 the then Crawley manager, Fred Cunnell, signed the ex-Spurs keeper and the Legend was born.

In the next five seasons Stan was to play 67 first team games for the Red Devils, whether it was for Crawley FC 1956-58 or for Crawley Town 1958-1961, but that was not even the start of the "Mr Crawley Town" story.

In his first season, with Crawley FC playing in Red and White hoops, Stan started in the reserves, but after just four first team games played, he replaced John Fairhead in goal and remained there for the rest of the season, accruing thirty-one appearances. Fifteen of these would have been witnessed by yours truly in my first season accompanying my dad, Bob, to home games at Town Meadow. In fact, we lost the first four games of the season against Tonbridge reserves, Guildford, Windsor and Luton A. The last being by five nil at home, which probably prompted the change in goalkeeper. The inclusion of Stan certainly paid immediate dividends as we won the next three games, including a seven-nil demolition of Brighton A. Playing against the A sides of West Ham and Chelsea and the reserve teams of more established non-league sides was always going to be a huge step-up from the Sussex County League and the season ended with Crawley in 14th place out of 18, having won nine, drawn seven and lost eighteen, scoring sixty-one goals whilst conceding seventy-five.

The next season saw an improvement, with Crawley moving up to 11[th,] with Stan sharing the goalkeeping duties with Pat Dowling almost on a fifty-fifty basis. For the second year running we finished above Brighton, with them finishing bottom of the league.

The next three seasons, now under the name of Crawley Town, saw the club's fortunes on the field suffer, with 14th, 20th (bottom) and 17th place finishes. This coincided with Stan featuring just another twenty times in the first team, but the club did manage to appear in the Sussex Senior Cup final in 1958/59, losing by two goals to one against Worthing at the Goldstone Ground with Pat Dowling in goal.

Stan was then offered the Manager's job in 1960 but at the age of just 34 he didn't feel ready to take on that responsibility and, just one year later, he hung up his boots and gloves (if he wore any) because of a bad back injury.

Stan's playing days were over, but his service to the Club was just beginning.

At the time of Stan's forced retirement from playing he was just 35, three years younger than Glenn "the cat" Morris. Stan, however, did not go quietly into the night of retirement. To the contrary, he raged against the extinguishing of his playing light and took up several roles at the club which he did not relinquish until Crawley Town moved to the Broadfield stadium in 1997

These roles included stints as youth team manager, chief scout, grounds man, first team manager and a remarkable 30 years as General Secretary of the club.

Among those players he brought into the club whilst scouting were Ray Carter, Eric Whitington, John Maggs, Dave Haining and Vic Bragg and a quick walk down memory lane shows what a good judge of playing ability and character Stan was.

Ray Carter, a West Hoathly lad, who originally played for factory side APV, tried his luck playing league football, first for Torquay United and then Exeter City. But Stan used his scouting ability, along with the lure of a job in a sports shop and a house in the developing New Town, to get him to Crawley where he was signed by then manager Fred Cook for the beginning of the 1963/64 season, our first in the Southern League Division 1. In the next three seasons he went on to score 57 goals for the Red Devils.

John Maggs also signed in 1963 and went on to play over 700 times for Crawley Town. Most of those games were in goal, but he did also play a few games up front towards the end of his playing career, before becoming Manager and Chairman of the club. Two big ticks against Stan's scouting ability as both players, in my opinion, would be in the top three in their respective positions in a Crawley Town role of most valuable players.

Outside of football, the Markham family had settled into the New Town well, and in 1965, their third child, a second daughter, was born. The local paper made the following announcement, "we scored a hat-trick at Town Meadow this week without kicking a ball. By this I mean a hat-trick of births, not goals. Congratulations were in order for 'A' Team Manager Stan Markham, Secretary Len Groom and centre-half Glyn Jones. I guess that's another three more on our gate, all gratefully accepted". Indeed, just one-week later John Maggs' wife, Janet, gave birth to their daughter and Janet and Alma were together in the same maternity ward at Crawley hospital. Yes, babies were born in Crawley back then! The arrival of his daughter obviously did not put Stan off doing the right thing for Crawley Town as it was in 1965, he scouted a certain forward, who himself was to become a Crawley Town legend. I am, of course, referring to Dave "Rubberman" Haining. Stan invited Dave for a trial after seeing him play for local side Crawley United. He played over 500 games for the club, scoring eighty goals and had five separate spells as manager or caretaker manager between 1974 and 1996, taking over the role of Club Secretary upon Stan's retirement in 1997. Another credit for Stan "Mr. Crawley Town" Markham

Having turned down the chance to be Crawley Town manager in 1960 he reluctantly took up the challenge in 1970 and 1974 upon the incumbent managers' resignations as a report from 1970 shows.

"He has taken over the duties, a quiet but hardworking club man, Markham is a shrewd judge of the game and well-versed in Town's problems".

The problems being that those running the club had full-time jobs and fitted in club duties around them, mostly for love and not money. With no cash, low gate receipts, the club buildings falling into disarray and a quagmire for a pitch, the manager's job was a thankless task. However, before Stan's first period at the helm in 1970, Crawley Town under the management of Roy Jennings had won promotion to the 5th level of English football for the first time in their history. In those days there wasn't a Conference, and the 5th level was represented by the Southern League Premier Division and the Northern Premier League, with promotion to the football league being through election......if you were lucky! More often than not, the Football League blazers would re-elect their bottom club rather than welcome new boys into their club.

Nonetheless, to get to that level was significant for a club at our level and was down to the management of Roy Jennings and the scouting ability of our Stan. Vic Bragg was one of the players brought in by Stan at the beginning of the 1968-69 season, who went on to win promotion that year and end up making over 600 appearances before retiring in 1983. Vic then went on to have a career as a teacher and to work for Brighton and Hove Albion and manage England Under 18s in 2002.

Going back to the 1969-70 season, with Jennings as manager and Stan as Club Secretary, Town started the season with a four two home win over Kings Lynn, but this proved to be a false dawn as we won only five more games that season, and were relegated back from whence we had come with just 27 points accrued (33 in today's money). The season also saw two heavy defeats at Plough Lane against the non-plastic Wimbledon (9-0) and at the Abbey stadium in Cambridge against United (8-0). In January 1970 Roy Jennings resigned and Stan Markham stepped into the breach for the first time but was unable to prevent the inevitable and back to the first division we dropped.

So, Stan was now Manager, Secretary and Grounds man and during his two-year stint in charge saw a fair amount of success, guiding us to 10th and 4[th,] losing out on promotion in 1972 by just four points. In both seasons we were the division's leading scorers, with 84 from 38 games in 1971 and 67 from 30 in 1972. He was also the first manager to get Crawley Town into the First-round proper of the FA Cup, not just once but twice.

Stan's two impressive cup runs started in the first week of September 1970 when Crawley, along with another 511 teams, took place in the First qualifying round. The first three rounds saw Crawley progress against Haywards Heath and Woking at home by 3-1 and 3-0 respectively, followed by an emphatic four nil victory away to Carshalton Athletic. For the second year running we were drawn away from home in the fourth round, this time to Folkestone, and for the second year running Crawley forced a replay with another nil nil draw. This year though, Stan would lead us over the final hurdle. With the replay poised at two all and with Crawley kicking up the slope toward the West Bank, Colin Blaber stormed up the pitch, before unleashing an unstoppable shot from the edge of the penalty area which won the tie, thus making history. The excitement in the crowd that night saw the concrete wall behind the goal collapse, spilling fans into the back of the net. Luckily, nothing but pride was seriously hurt. Folkestone would go on to win promotion to the Southern League Premier Division.

The draw for the next round, the First Round Proper, saw us pitted against a team who would finish the season just six points behind the eventual Southern League Champions, Yeovil Town. They were of course, Chelmsford City. The Red devils were just seven minutes away from a second-round tie against Third division (League 1 in 2022 terminology) Torquay United when Pat Ferry, a London Taxi driver by trade, broke red hearts by equalising at the Fire station end of Town Meadow.

The replay, just two days later, saw the run come to a heroic end, with goalkeeper John Maggs playing most of the game with a broken hand, and with Crawley succumbing by six goals to one. The Observer reported that Chelmsford were vastly improved from the first game and included this reference to Stan in their report "Crawley lost the game in the first 15 minutes and, as manager Stan Markham said afterwards, it was the first two goals that did the damage". To add insult to injury, the supporter's coach had its windows smashed as it left the ground, and on a bitterly cold November night had to travel back to Crawley open to the elements.

The next season saw an almost carbon copy run and after beating Eastbourne Town, East Grinstead and Horsham comfortably we drew nil nil at the Pilot field against Hastings United, before dispatching them, as we did with Folkestone, by three goals to two in another pulsating match at Town Meadow. This year our reward was our first encounter, in a competitive match, against a Football League side, Exeter City.

Unfortunately, history was to repeat itself, with Phil Basey missing a great chance to put us through just before full time at Town Meadow, and the Grecians beating us by two goals to nil at St James Park.

After Stan's first stint as Manager the Club appointed Tony Elkins-Green as first team coach, with Stan continuing as Club Secretary alongside other duties such as youth team manager, chief scout and grounds man. He also returned to First team management in 1974 when Tony Elkins-Green departed the club until John Maggs took over the reins in the 80s. In his time as Secretary, he worked alongside 15 different managers or acting managers, with 13 of them in the 1990s alone, albeit with some of them, such as Dave Haining and John Maggs having more than one go.

The one person who was a constant at that time was our Stan. Whether it was making sure the pitch didn't resemble a World War 1 Battlefield, Secretary duties or anything that needed doing, Stan, along with a dedicated group of supporters endeavoured against all the odds to ensure games were played and the club kept on going. An article in the Times Herald on 24th January 1969 describes the frustration and dejection that settled over Town Mead when the game against Gravesend was washed out for the 2nd time in 5 days. "From lunch time a small band of dedicated fans tried to mop up surface water with sacking and old clothes. But even as they wrung out their efforts in a tin bath the rain continued to fall steadily, and they had to admit defeat. In the worst spots liquid mud was up to eight inches deep". And at Town Mead this was far from a rare occasion - an interview in the Crawley & District Observer on 17th April 1970 records that Bruce Winfield, Alan Pocock and Dennis Lovell "spent hours trying to get the pitch just right – it destroys them when they see the result of all their labours". Others that helped on match days to get the pitch ready were Nick Hilton, Jim Baker and Johnnie Button, all of whom still support the club to this day.

The fact that we got through the 70s owes a lot to the dedication of Stan and his band of helpers and indeed other stalwarts as the club was running at a loss of over £100 per week due to high wages, poor gates, an inadequate tote income and little cash flow from the Floodlight Club. Few of the directors were seen at Town Mead and the time had come for those with neither the time nor the effort to devote to the club to pull out. Relying on young local players playing in front of crowds around 700 Crawley faced re-election three times in the decade, and the fact that we were re-elected must surely be, in some part, down to the respect that the Southern League had for our Club Secretary.

As with others involved with the club, Stan himself had a full-time job. His job was at Upjohn Pharmaceutical, and after an early shift at work, finishing at 2pm, it was down to Town Mead as there was always something that needed doing for love, not money. It would be interesting to know the number of miles that Stan must have covered over the pitch during his time at Town Mead, whilst playing and then sowing the grass seed, cutting the grass, rolling the pitch and painstakingly marking out the white lines, all come rain, sunshine, sleet and snow, alongside the family dog, Kate, who was always there by his side. He even had to manually insert the wooden tiles on the fixture board that overlooked Ifield Avenue to advertise the upcoming game.

In 1975 he even found the time and energy to manage the local Upjohn football team when they travelled to Belgium and won the whole inter-company tournament.

Stan's personal ambition was that Crawley Town should reach the final of the FA Trophy and play at Wembley. Alas that never happened, but his proudest moment was yet to come.......and in the 1983/84 season, working as club secretary, he saw his beloved Crawley Town win promotion back to the Southern League Premier Division, but unlike the last time this had been achieved, this was now tier 6 of the pyramid, following the introduction of the Alliance Premier League aka Conference aka National League in 1979.

He formally retired from Upjohn in 1991, and to mark the occasion Terry Venables sent him a letter wishing him well in his retirement years. Spurs also arranged for him to take four of his family to see the Manchester United game on New Year's Day in 1996.

In 1997 he stepped down from his role as Club Secretary, receiving a long service award from the Southern League in recognition of his fantastic effort and loyalty and becoming a Vice-President at Crawley Town. His retirement coincided with the club's move to Broadfield, but somebody forgot to tell him he had retired, as he played a vital role in getting a "new" secretary au fait with all the regulations and procedures. That man was, of course, another legend, Dave Haining. Stan also found time to visit the stadium every Tuesday and Thursday, when he would be seen, up a ladder, changing the fixture board by the roundabout.

In his time as Club Secretary, Crawley Town not only won promotion into the Southern League Premier twice, but also had success in numerous cup competitions such as the County Cups (Professional, Senior and Floodlit), the Gilbert Rice Floodlit Cup and the Roy Hayden Trophy, all of which gave him an enormous amount of pride.

Sadly, in 2002 he was taken ill, which called a halt to him attending matches. However, aided by Ian Hands, he kept abreast of how the Red Devils were faring, and in his final years must surely have been cheered by our Southern League Cup victory. Unfortunately, he never got to see us do the double, as, whilst waiting in St George's hospital for a hip operation, he contracted

Pneumonia and sadly left us on the 5th August 2003, surrounded by his family, at five to eight in the evening

The very next evening, Crawley played a Tottenham Hotspur X1 in a friendly, which was attended by a large contingent of his family who really appreciated the way the Crawley faithful respected the minutes silence for a great man.

At Stan's funeral the hearse drove to Broadfield Stadium and made a circuit around the pitch and Bill Nicholson sent flowers from Tottenham, a sign of how much he was loved by both clubs

However, there was a lot more to "Stan the Man" than football. He was very much a family man and a wonderful father to three children and a doting grandfather to five grandchildren. At 6'3" he was a gentle giant; honest and fair, a rock to rely on and very caring and supportive. He embraced gardening and nature, enjoyed James Bond films and loved watching tennis at Wimbledon and he was a nifty pool player to boot. He would stand tall as he proudly donned his Club blazer and Old Spice aftershave, critically straightening his tie, before attending a formal CTFC or Southern League event. He had no desire to travel abroad claiming he had seen more than enough during the war, but he was more than happy to spend time on the south coast in England, sporting the tan accrued through endless hours of working on the Town Mead pitch.

Stan Markham, goalkeeper, husband, father and grandfather. A true gentleman and legend of the club.

Chapter Three

The Bulman Years

If you had to ask a cross section of today's Crawley Town fans who should be thought of as a legend, I am absolutely positive that Dannie Bulman would be chosen by people of all ages, genders and races. I have to confess, that Dannie has always featured high in the Leake and Humphrey households ranking of Crawley players, ever since his arrival back in 2006. He has always given his all, both on and off the pitch, for the club he has grown to love. Indeed, when asked "what percentage of him is a red?" his answer was :

"Wellllll. I'm a Chelsea boy. but I'm a Crawley Man that's for sure. So to answer your question, I'm 100% RED!!"

Born on the 24th January 1979 in the town of Ashford , Surrey (historically Middlesex) he played for his school and, in his own words, "Yeah played for my school, won a few cup finals. Played at college too and scored from the kick off in one game". At the age of 15 he was signed by Ashford (Middlesex), evidently a confident fifteen year old who stayed there for four years until signed, at the age of 19 , by Wycombe Wanderers, then in the second division, which is now known as EFL 1. He attracted a fee of £10000, and was the first player ever to leave Ashford's Short Lane ground for the Football League. The fee was a record at the time involving a Combined Counties League club, and Ashford's website pays this tribute to him.

"Dannie's legacy is a significant one, as the fee helped the club to construct the Main Stand."

Dannie became a folk hero at Wycombe Wanderers, when he scored on his debut. Now Crawley fans will remember Dannie for thunderous efforts, like the one against Colchester United in the Carabao Cup (when he shouldn't have been playing) or the brace against our friends from Kingston (a game which I missed) but I'll let Wikipedia and the Ashford and Wycombe websites describe that first goal for the chairboys.

"Bulman made his debut as a late substitute in a 1–1 draw at home to Bristol Rovers on 31 August 1998, and within 15 seconds of coming on the pitch, he scored as Lee Jones' clearance had deflected off his buttocks and into the net"

Wikipedia

"He became a cult hero among the Wanderers faithful after scoring on his debut with his first touch... which was off his backside!

Ashford Town (Middlesex)

"WYCOMBE v BRISTOL ROVERS

Monday 31st August 1998- Division Two

There may not have been many people there to see it but Danny Bulman's backside helped Wycombe claim their first League point of the season. An 84th minute goal by Barry Hayles had given Rovers a deserved lead and as many Wycombe fans were wondering where the next goal, let alone point was coming from Bulman's fluke made it a never to be forgotten Football League debut. The enthusiastic youngster blocked a clearance from Rover's keeper Lee Jones during the third minute of injury time and the ball rolled into the empty net to delight the loyal Wycombe fans who had stayed to the end."

Wycombe Wanderers FC

Over the next six years Dannie played 202 games for the Chairboys and scored 12 goals, one of which, we know, was scored off his posterior. That, however, does not do justice to his time at Adams Park. From 1998 to 2004, he served under five managers. Starting with Neil Smillie, who signed him, he actually had three in his first season, with Terry Evans replacing Smillie, but only being in charge for a month before Lawrie Sanchez took over towards the end of the season. Sanchez brought some stability to the Chair boys and remained there until the September of Dannie's last season at the club. For most of the time that Dannie was there, Wycombe were a comfortable midtable team but in his last two years they had fallen to 18th and eventually were relegated to the bottom tier of the football League which coincided with Dannie's departure at the end of his six-year contract. The manager at the time was ex-Arsenal and England centre back Tony Adams, but wasn't he the player who once applauded the mural at the north Bank, Highbury? What does he know, eh?

A not very successful time, you might say, but that would be to ignore the 2000-2001 season in which Wycombe became one of the few third tier clubs to reach the semi-finals of the FA Cup. The run to the semi-final started in the First-round proper against Harrow Borough with a three-nil win, but Dannie's first appearance in the cup that season wasn't until the second round when Second Division (League 1) Millwall were defeated in a replay at Adams Park. Grimsby, Wolves and Wimbledon (the real one), all First division (Championship) clubs were all beaten in the next three rounds taking the Chair Boys through to the quarter final against Premier League Leicester City at their old Filbert Street ground. However, it was in the Wimbledon tie when Dannie really came to the fore. Wycombe were drawn at home and had to come back from two down to force a replay at Selhurst Park (Plough Lane was no more). In the replay they went behind early on but then Dannie, on a sortie into the box, saw his shot deflected into the path of Dave Carroll who slotted home the equaliser. Despite having a penalty saved in normal time, the Dons re-established their lead early into extra time and looked to be going through in the dying seconds. But cometh the hour cometh the Man, the Bulman. Another shot, or was it a pass, found McCarthy who levelled and took the game to penalties. The shoot-out was won by Wycombe by eight goals to seven, including Wycombe's third, taken emphatically by Dannie and ending in the top right-hand corner of the net.

In the next round it was time for Dannie to make the acquaintance of Robbie "can't get into the Broadfield" Savage but Wycombe were running on empty as far as forward players were concerned, and special measures had to be taken.

Next up for Dannie in his Wycombe career was a game that I remember well myself, but at the time, it being BB (before Bullie) in Crawley terms, I never really appreciated how much he contributed to Wycombe's FA cup run and have to wonder now how we were lucky enough to see him wear the red of Crawley Town. The quarter final, against Leicester City, saw Wycombe, ironically, playing in a kit very similar to the red and white quarters worn by Crawley FC between the second world war and the adoption of "Town" into our name. However, what caught the imagination of the general public was that Wycombe, had lost all six of their contracted forwards to injury, and had been forced to advertise on Ceefax* for non-contracted forwards to come to their rescue. Cue the arrival of Roy Essandoh ten days before the game, Sanchez gave him the benefit of the doubt and included him on the bench for the quarter final.

Starting with midfielder Ryan up front, alongside on loan striker Clegg, Wycombe kept Leicester at bay in the first twenty minutes, but the tide started to turn when Dannie Bulman nearly caught out Royce with a 25-yard shot that almost crept in at the near post, and just a few moments later one of Bullie's crosses was headed over by Clegg. The game then got a little heated thanks to the Steve Brown v Robbie Savage battle, which saw them both receive yellow cards just eight minutes apart before half time.

One all at half time, the 3000 Chairboys in the 21000 crowd were rewarded in the fiftieth minute, when midfielder McCarthy headed home a free kick to put them one up, but in 68th minute Izzet equalised and for a little while it looked as if the Premier League side would prevail over the minnows. Lawrie Sanchez, in the 74th minute, made the substitution that would prove crucial, bringing on Castledine and Essandoh for the tiring Ryan and Clegg, only to be banished to the stands six minutes later for running 50 yards down the touch line to protest the non-awarding of a penalty for a Stefan Oakes handball. Many people will remember the television coverage showing Sanchez watching the remainder of the game on a tv set in the tunnel, but what was lost to me at the time was who delivered the crucial cross to send Wycombe to a Villa Park Semi-final against Liverpool. In the 93rd minute of the game, a free kick from the left was punched out by Royce in the City goal, but only to Dannie Bulman, who sent a looping cross in to the box, which was headed back into the path of Essandoh, by Bates, who headed into the top corner for a famous victory. In the celebrations that ensued, Steve Brown received his second card for removing his shirt which is probably the only time a non-scorer has been punished for this terrible crime against humanity.

2004 saw Dannie come to the end of his contract at Wycombe Wanderers, and, in order to stay close to his home, he signed for Stevenage, who at the time were managed by ex-Red (although not mentioned on Wikipedia) Graham Westley.

In that first season at Broadhall, the other new towners made the Conference Play-off final, played at the Britannia (now the Bet 365) stadium, where Dannie, alongside Justin Gregory, came away with a loser's medal after they lost one nil to Carlisle. Perhaps, if they had won that game the Red Devil Bulman might never have been. He stayed with Stevenage until 2006 when Dannie came to Broadfield Stadium for the first time and the manager, who we all love to hate, moved to Rushden and Diamonds. His stay in Hertfordshire saw him make 80 appearances and score three goals, and he was loaned out to Crawley in 2006, signing on "permanently" at the beginning of the 2007/09 season.

He very soon became a favourite with the Red Devil supporters and, it was with considerable disappointment in the fan base that, he left us after two-and-a-half seasons, having played 126 games scoring 9 goals in the process. His new club, Oxford United (your stadium only has three sides) reached the Conference play-off final in his first season, this time at the new Wembley Stadium. In his team, that day, was another Ex Red, Jake Wright, and opposing them was a certain Richard Brodie, playing in the Red and White of York City. The game went Oxford's way by three goals to one with well- known names Matt Green, James Constable and Alfie Potter scoring the United goals. His stay at the Manor Ground saw him make 47 appearances but Oxford were the only club who failed to see him score a goal.

Dannie returned to Crawley on loan in September 2010, before signing on his second permanent contract with the club in January 2011. As we, Crawley Town fans, will know, this season saw him win his second Conference promotion in two years, but this time it was destined to be the Championship winning season under the management of Steve Evans. That record season only being surpassed in 2023 by Wrexham FC.

The historical importance of that season, for Crawley fans, should be etched on their brains and in their hearts, but for me the most significant Dannie related moments, in that season of seasons, were his twelve yard strike to open the scoring away to Mansfield in a four - one win, and his delightful pass at Football League Torquay which saw Matt Tubbs score, to send us, as it proved the day after, to Old Trafford.

It seems that Sam Elliott , I think of the Crawley Observer, also believed Dannie's performance at the Theatre of Dreams also stood out, as in his player ratings, this is what he wrote:

"Dannie Bulman, passing couldn't be faulted and performed the holding role like he has done superbly in the Blue Square Premier League. Didn't flinch when up against the Premier League's finest – even Wayne Rooney , sitting deep, was kept in check"

Just don't agree with Sam's score of 7/10, surely a 9 at least.

Following on from the excitement of the Conference winning season, Dannie was to play over 100 more games for Crawley Town, before leaving at the end of the 2013/14 season to join our dear friends from Kingston. In his time with us in that second spell, he played 147 games scoring five goals and unfortunately, I missed what was probably his best performance during that time.

The date was 22nd October 2011, and I was missing in action due to a pre-arranged family trip. Whilst away I was kept up to date with the goings on at, what was once the home of Kingstonians, Kingsmeadow. Perhaps it was this game that got the plastics interested in his signature. The game started really well for Crawley Town with an Andy Drury corner being sliced into his own net by a Wimbledon defender on two minutes and Claude Davis scoring with a header from another Drury corner just seven minutes later putting the reds two up and cruising. However, the Dons hit back with two of their own before the break and the two teams went in level. The second half, however, saw the Devils regain the initiative with a 54th minute penalty, hit high into the goal by Matt Tubbs, and a header from Dannie Bulman five minutes later to regain the two-goal lead. This goal was made and finished by Dannie after some fine interplay with John Akinde, but the goal which sealed the win came in the 84th minute when Dannie completed his first ever brace in professional football, bullet heading a fine cross from Scott Neilson into the net to signal a mass exodus from the ground by the home support, accompanied by a rousing rendition of "Is there a fire drill" from the travelling reds. AND I MISSED IT.

As mentioned earlier, Dannie left the Broadfield at the end of the 2013/2014 season and thus avoided our relegation from League One in 2014/2015, himself stepping down into League Two to feature alongside George Francomb, Adebayo Akinfenwa and another Reds favourite, Matt Tubbs, on loan from Bournemouth. Scoring just one goal in that season, Dannie helped AFC Wimbledon reach the third-round of the FA Cup, beating York City before overcoming his old club Wycombe Wanderers to gain the reward of facing Liverpool for the second time.

Steven Gerard scored a brace which saw Liverpool triumphant by two goals to one, but George Francomb provided the corner from which Akinfenwa equalised and Dannie saw one of his trademark shots go narrowly over the bar at two one. Not many players from the lower reaches of the league get to play Liverpool once, let alone twice. Even fewer get to do it with the style and commitment shown by Bully.

31

The 2015/16 season saw Dannie return to the Broadfield, but this time as an opponent, and sad to say, from a Red point of view, was triumphant as AFC did the double over Crawley on their way to reaching the League 2 play off final, after finishing 7th in the League.

After beating Accrington Stanley in the semi-final, Dannie then played in the final at Wembley against Plymouth Argyle where Wimbledon were triumphant by two goals to nil.

In spite of winning the Players' Player of the Year award for AFC in the 2016/2017 season he was, rather strangely, released by them at the end of their first season in League 1. As a sign of how much fans at whatever club he played for appreciated him and his on field efforts, Dannie was selected as part of AFC Wimbledon's team of the decade for the 2010s. Where else should he go, but back to his spiritual home, here at Broadfield, where he would stay until his retirement in April 2022. During his final period with Crawley Town he played another 108 games and scored three times. This brought his career totals to 831 games played and 38 goals scored, with those played and scored in a "red" shirt numbering 381 and 17 respectively.

From 2017 until his retirement in 2022 he signed year long contracts and became the oldest active player in the English Football League during the 2019/2020 season at the age of 40, ahead of Kevin Ellison, James Coppinger and Aaron Wilbraham.

His last three goals, scored in that last time at Broadfield, were scored on the 24th of November 2018 against Crewe, the 6th April 2019 against the vegemite sandwich brigade from Nailsworth and on the 7th November 2019 against Colchester United in the League Cup.

The first of those goals, all of which were scored at the Broadfield, came in the 95th minute of the game against Crewe and was the third goal in a three nil victory. One sided? Yes it was, Crewe played us off the park and Glenn Morris was awarded player of the match by yours truly and Jim Hyton. In those days, however, we took our chances well and Dannie's goal was recorded as a simple tap in from a Lewis Young cross.

The other goals were scored by Josh Payne, from the spot and Joe McNerney.

The second and third of those three goals were both wonderful drives from distance, the first from fully 30 yards against Forest Green Rovers in a two one home defeat and the second from 25 yards in the three one defeat that ended our wonderful run in the League Cup against Colchester United. The run that had seen us claim our first Premier League scalp against Norwich City and beat Stoke City on penalties.

The day after the Colchester United game, the draw paired them with Manchester United at Old Trafford, but the disappointment was tempered by the realisation that, even if we had won the night before, we would have been chucked out of the competition for fielding two players who should have been suspended. One of them being Dannie Bulman our goal scorer.

In his last season of actually playing at Crawley Town he played only a handful of games, but one of them was the incredible rematch against Torquay United in the FA Cup which saw Crawley Town come back repeatedly to win by six goals to five.

On 2 April 2022, Bulman announced his retirement from professional football at the age of 43 and the End of Season Awards evening was held in his honour, and a very professional and successful career came to an end.

The next few pages are seen through Dannie's eyes and were responses to questions posed by myself. They are written, with a little license, but without the questions. You're Crawley Fans, you'll work it out.

I was born on the 24th January 1979 in Ashford, Middlesex, and I am married to my gorgeous amazing wife Emily and have a daughter Jolie aged 19 and a son Luciano, aged 5. As for my time at school, they can't teach what I have.

I first came to Crawley in August 2006, when we were playing in the Football Conference. At the time I joined, Vic Marley was chairman under the ownership of Chas and Mohammed Azwar

Majeed. Vic was the first face I saw when coming through the door, what a lovely genuine man, Legend.

Chas was the only owner I met, and I had many meetings with him over the hardship the club was going through. We actually had my contract negotiations over a fish finger sandwich in one of his restaurants.

The man, the legend who first bought me to the club was John Hollins, what a guy!! A true gentleman, he was forever smiling in the face of diversity.

After he left the club John Yems became caretaker manager aided by player/managers Ben Judge and David Woozley. What a trio!! The two players and I formed a great bond. I would drive in with Wooz and was forever chatting with Judgey, usually over a beer or two. Mr Yems was great, and this was the reason why I put his name forward when the manager's job came up at Crawley later on down the road.(After Gaby Cioffe). In my opinion he was a fantastic man manager, who really knew how to get the best out of what he had at his disposal.

When I'm talking about what I think of other players I have played with, the most important consideration for me is their character. If you have a great presence within the changing room then you are invaluable to the team. Throughout my time at the club I have come across many players, too many to mention, but here I go.

For me I have to name Matt Tubbs obviously, my mate, my goal scorer, my brother from another mother.

John Dempster, without doubt the funniest person I have come across, not only in football but in my life.

Scott Shearer, my big stinky cuddly Scottish bear. I love this guy, drove in with him for years and he is a true gentle giant. Heart of gold.

Scott Neilson, biggest and best cannon I've ever met. He is your "go to" for a night out.

Josh Simpson, captain marvel. Great guy with an unbelievable sense of humour.

Kyle McFadzean, what a player. Such a strong bugger. Could have played a lot higher if his health issue hadn't put an end to a move to a club, now in the premier league.(Now with Coventry City)

The game which stands out for me the most in my time at Crawley has to be, I think, the last game of the season at Accrington Stanley to get promoted to League 1. Basically the wheels had well and truly come off of our Promotion push and we were hanging on to 3rd spot. Steve had jumped ship to Rotherham, we lost the previous game something like 4-1 at home to a very good Crewe Team. (In fact it was three nil at home to Hereford United, who eventually were relegated, both games against Crewe that year were one all draws, no one's perfect Dannie) Confidence was low, momentum had stopped and started to go backwards. So the feeling when that final whistle blew, of sheer elation, was very overwhelming. We did it!! We don't know how or why but we did it!!! (Might have had something to do with the support) Next stop the booze bus home for an absolute mammoth session that lasted a few days.

One funny story that I can recall that isn't too blue is; we were away with Crawley for some hot weather training. We had the afternoon off so we decided to venture to the local supermarket for some home comforts. The manager at the time was Steve Evans!! We all rocked back to the hotel and back to our rooms to eat our weight in sugary junk food. Steve was far too busy (lazy) to go. Steve started getting a wee bit peckish. Steve wanted gums!!(Scottish word for sweets I believe.) He called the room of youth player Byron Napper and demanded he goes round the players' rooms to acquire said Gums. Byron, in his naivety knocked on Mr Cannons door (Scotty Neilson). Big error!! First he politely asked Byron to remove himself from the room (basically F*&%K OFF). But before Byron could vacate, Mr Neilson's devilish mind started to tick as he was munching on some Maltesers! He decided to carefully bite the chocolate from the Maltesers leaving just the spheroid malted milk centre and replace them back in the back. Silly Byron went along with this offering for Steve while filming the whole event. Steve hit the roof like only Steve can and demanded that players should be more respectful, also gave us a double training session that evening. Steve being Steve, in the same breath, laughed it off.

The most memorable member of the backroom staff was Mark Stein!!! He was a Chelsea Legend in my eyes, but to others he was a very, very average, at best, Physio! No matter if you broke a toe, broke a finger, cut head or dislocated your spine he would ask you to do the same test to assess you, which would usually have you walking round the physio room like some sort of animal. Would have been hilarious if he wasn't actually serious.

The feeling of being promoted is unbeatable, so many different emotions all happening at once. Relief, joy! A release of all the seasons hard work ending in triumph. Our day out at Old Trafford was all great, but at the end of the day we lost. Underneath it all I'm a winner, so when that final whistle goes and you have lost I'm dying inside. I put a brave face on it but the tears of a clown, if you will.

I'm a Chelsea boy at heart, but I'm a Crawley Man that's for sure. So to answer every Crawley fan's question I'm 100% RED!!

Chapter Four

BAME, Breaking down the barriers

The world we live in consists of all types of people; happy, sad, peaceful, angry, simple, complicated, selfish and altruistic. Hence the saying "It takes all sorts ...". You will hopefully notice that I have made no reference to nationalities, creeds or colours, and that is because, for me, these are the least important characteristics to be taken into consideration when valuing someone's contribution to life in general and football in particular.

This chapter has not been prompted by events that have occurred inside or outside our club in the recent past, but rather by the need to acknowledge the contribution made by players from a BAME background. Inevitably there will be players that don't get a mention but hopefully I will cover the ones remembered by the majority of fans with the most fondness.

It is fair to say that black players had been playing professional football since its very beginning (Arthur Warton, 1886-1902) but, before the 1970s, the most exotic places that Crawley FC and Crawley Town recruited their players from, would have been from other counties in England and some from as far afield as Wales, Scotland and even Ireland. However, following the Second World War and the coming of the New Town and the necessary influx of people from the commonwealth to help us rebuild our nation, the pool of players available grew enormously.

The first player of a BAME background that I can remember playing for the first team was Trevor Smith. He signed at the beginning of the 1978/79 season and stayed with us until the end of our 1983/84 season making 73 appearances, including four as substitute and scored a total of seven goals from, as far as I can remember, a right-wing position. The importance of his last season with us was that we won promotion back to the Southern League Premier Division that year, but, unlike our promotion in 1969, it did not take us to the top of the non-league pyramid as The Alliance Premier had been formed, back in 1979, from the top Southern League Premier and Northern Premier League teams. In 1986 it was renamed the Football Conference and, after we had won it in 2011, became the National League in 2015. Back to Trevor, I remember him as a tricky ball playing forward, and being a Smith, obviously inherited the nick name Smudger.

However, Trevor's claim to being the first BAME player to don the red shirt must come with the "1st First Team player" tag as Keith Rego played for Crawley Town reserves back in 1971/72, as can be seen in the picture of the reserves before a home match against Pagham at Town mead. Keith is pictured in the front row next to Crawley Town legend Dave Haining. This would be about the same time as Brendan Batson signed for Arsenal. Between the days of Keith Rego, Trevor Smith and our current team we have had numerous players of a BAME background, numbering at least 125 since 1970. I can't hope to do justice to all these players in this book, so I am going to concentrate on those who, in my opinion, have had the biggest impact on the memory cells of Crawley Town supporters.

Whilst watching the English Roses winning against New Zealand in the Women's Rugby Union World Cup Final, my phone rang with a number I did not recognise. I answered, and forgot all about the Rugby, as I realised it was Keith Rego responding to a Facebook message, I had sent him. We lost the Rugby in the end, but the time I spent talking to Keith was worth it, to say the least.

Keith spent his childhood in South London and moved, with his family, to Crawley in the sixties. He admits to having a short fuse when on the football pitch, and recalls being sent off "a couple of times". Having played for both Ifield and APV, he played for Crawley Town Reserves under the legend Dave Haining, and remembers one game where his colour was questioned. Playing on the wing, the opposing full back kept calling him a w*g. Keith answered this by nutmegging the defender and chipping the onrushing keeper, the ball ending up in the top corner of the net. As Keith made his way back into his own half for the game to restart, he passed the full back and said, "Not bad for a w*g, eh?".

Supporting Aston Villa, whilst his brothers followed West Ham, Keith had trials with Chelsea but played most of his football in local leagues, both here in Sussex and in South London. He remembers playing in one game against Brighton reserves, leading five three but eventually losing six five because of the introduction of Peter Ward and Tony Towner.

Going on from Keith and Trevor, the next BAME players I remember are Merrick Harriott and Ron De Souza. Merrick was an old-fashioned centre forward, whilst Ron De Souza played in goal. Merrick made 43 appearances, 32 in the league, 11 in Cup matches and scored 15 goals, 9 in the league and 6 in cup games. He played alongside a true Red Devil legend, Brian Gregory and was fundamental in seeing Crawley rise from 21st in 1982 to 7th by the end of the 1982-83 season. He scored one goal in a six two friendly win against Billingshurst at the beginning of our promotion season in 1983-84 but left soon afterwards, being replaced in the side by Jeff Wood.

Ron De Souza, I believe, is the first player of a BAME background to play in goal for Crawley Town, playing fifteen times, nine in the league and six in cup games, and keeping seven clean sheets in the process.

The next player, who played over two seasons for Crawley Town back in 1995 and 1996, that sticks in my memory is one Raphael Meade. We first came across Raph, however, back in 1992 when we played for Brighton and Hove Albion in the third round of the FA Cup. He scored the fifth goal in our five-nil defeat in front of over 18000 spectators, as Crawley fans rued the fact that we hadn't played Tony Towner but were heartened by the fact that we had lasted longer in the cup than Arsenal, due to our game not kicking off until 315pm because of crowd congestion. Having started his career at Arsenal in 1977, he came to us at the ripe old age of 33, having played in Portugal, Spain, Scotland, Denmark and England, scoring goals wherever he went. For

Crawley, in seventy appearances, he scored 27 goals in both league and cup matches and was our leading scorer in the 1995/96 season before leaving for Sittingbourne part-way through the following year.

In the 1996/97 season we sat on just 35 points with only five games to play and were in grave danger of being relegated back to Southern League South, just before we were due to move to the Broadfield Stadium. We won the first of those five games at home to Dorchester by two nil, thanks to Johansen and Viv Jeffrey, but it was the next weekend that was to prove crucial in our fight against relegation, as we faced Kings Lynn away on the Saturday and Nuneaton Borough on the Sunday. I well remember both these games, as the first one was won by a late goal from another of our BAME heroes, Rodney Prosper, and was instrumental in me becoming Chair of the Supporters Club at the next AGM. But that's another story, suffice it to say that the jubilant reaction to the goal was not shared by all those purporting to be Crawley supporters that day. The next day, Jon Warden, signed on dual forms from Bromley that weekend, scored to beat the Borough and all of a sudden, we were on 44 points. The next Saturday, following our fourth win on the trot, against Atherstone United thanks to another Warden goal and a Craig Whitington penalty, we were able to leave Town Mead with heads held high, still in the Premier Division, although we did lose our final game away to Hastings Town.

Big Jon went on to score twenty-nine goals in League and Cup games for Crawley Town in 102 appearances and must surely be the only player that has scored a winning goal in a game and can also claim to have kept a clean sheet in the same match, after going in goal for an injured Colin Hunwick. The game was against Erith and Belvedere in a Southern League cup game in the 1998/99 season. Unfortunately, once before he had replaced Colin in goal, but we had lost by two goals to one at Bath City's Twerton Park.

Even fourteen years later he was keen to reminisce about his Crawley days when I met him at an FA Schools competition in Oxford where he was there with a team from Sittingbourne.

Alongside Jon Warden, came a young man who must merit as one of the most prolific goals scorers in the history of Crawley Town FC. His name was, and still is, Ben Abbey. During the 1997 to 1999 seasons, he made 97 appearances for our club, scoring 46 goals in the process. At the end of his second season with Crawley, I well remember going to see the Red Devils play at Eton Park, the then home of Burton Albion prior to their move to the Pirelli Stadium, and Ben scored the first goal in a two one victory. After the game, we stopped for a drink in Albion's social club, just outside the ground, where we chatted to some West Bromwich Albion supporters who had come to see Ben Abbey play, as rumours were rife that they were going to sign him. I think they talked to Tony Sweet for about ten minutes before they were told that he wasn't Ben Abbey. Some mischievous Crawley fans, identity withheld, silently sniggering into their pints whilst they chatted away. In the end, Ben, after cementing himself as a fans' favourite, signed for Oxford United for a fee of £30,000. There was a late bid from Exeter City, which would have been preferable for Crawley, who at the time were in administration, but the astute 21-year-old forward was reluctant to sign for them, saying "Oxford are a better club, playing in a higher league, and is a more convenient place to get to from my London home."

He retired from football in 2013, after having played for several clubs after Crawley, at the age of 36 having scored 121 goals in 342 appearances and went on to forge a successful career in Finance and Sports Management. At just 5ft 7inches (170cm for our younger readers) he reminded me of Phil Basey and Terry Robbins in his style of play, if not in appearance.

The next three players of a BAME background all featured in our 2003/2004 promotion winning season, you know the one, the one that really started our climb to where we are now. They are Francis Vines, Gavin Holligan and Nigel Brake.

Francis had scored 15 goals for the Red Devils before taking over as manager in January 2003 and within a season and a half had become the club's most successful manager, winning seven trophies culminating in promotion to the Football Conference for the first time in the club's history in 2003/2004. Two of his players, both of a BAME background were local lad, Nigel Brake, and former West Ham player Gavin Holligan. Gavin was at Crawley, on loan from Wycombe Wanderers, and scored 7 goals for us, the most important one, in my opinion, being the header away at Weymouth in our one nil win. I seem to remember that game being renowned for another reason, but I'll let Ian Payne remind you of that. He was released from Wycombe, as was Dannie "the legend "Bulman, by Tony Adams following his loan with us. Gavin retired in 2006, following a bad injury and went back to his musical career, which he had forsaken for football back in 1998, and has since become a successful singer/song writer.

Nigel Brake made 154 appearances in two spells for Crawley Town, scoring twenty goals across both League and Cup matches. In his second spell he won the Southern League title under Francis Vines

He is, of course, the son of another Crawley Town legend, Ann Brake, who has been a steward at the Broadfield since its' opening in 1997. In an article in the Argus back in December 2007 he had this to say about his mum.

"I'd have been retired a long time but for my mum. I wanted to pack it all in when I was about 19 or 20. I'd played County League football for Redhill, playing every week. The chance came to move to Carshalton who were playing about three levels above, the equivalent of Conference south. It was halfway through the season, and I struggled to get in the first team. ...…..

After a while I got a phone call from Cliff Cant who had just taken over at Crawley and he wanted me to go down there. But I didn't fancy it. That is where my mum came in. She pushed me into it. She told me that as I was sitting around doing nothing, I had nothing to lose. She has always supported me through thick and thin - and I don't argue with my mum! She encouraged me to start playing again and I owe it to her that that I am experiencing such great times now."

Nigel was playing for Horsham at the time and preparing for a second round FA Cup match against Swansea City, after having produced a contender for Goal of the Month on Match of the Day with his 30-yard thunderbolt that put Hornets on their way to a 4-1 victory in the first round against Maidenhead. Horsham held Swansea to a one all draw at Queen Street, before going down by six goals to two in the replay.

The match that I remember featuring one of Nigel's trademark pile drivers, was in November 1999 against Grantham at the Broadfield in front of 692 fans. Crawley, under Billy Smith at the time, stormed into a two-nil lead, but with just five minutes left, the score was two all, when Nigel volleyed home the winner from a Dean Green cross. This took the Red Devils off the bottom of the league, leap frogging Grantham in the process.

Mum was pleased.

The next four players of a BAME background I am going to write about take us through our Conference years to that wonderful season in 2010/2011 when we set a record, that has only just been surpassed..

First up, is John-Paul Pittman who played for Crawley between June 2007 and February 2009 when he was sold to Wycombe Wanderers for a five-figure fee. In this spell with the Red Devils, he made 60 appearances and scored 22 goals and became a favourite with the Red army.

JP made a short return to Crawley on an emergency loan in our first season in the Football League making another four appearances and scoring one goal. A goal, perhaps, that contributed greatly to our second promotion in two years.

You might also remember a game at the Broadfield when he was laid out on the ground for over twenty minutes after colliding with an over robust defender. I was on the microphone that day and was called down pitch side by Steve Evans, to keep people informed of his condition. He made a complete recovery after an anxious time laid static on the hallowed turf but was out with concussion for several games following the incident.

JP was born in Oklahoma City in 1986, where his dad was serving in the USAF at Tinker AFB, around about the same time as I was working there for Rediffusion Simulation on a simulator refurbishment, but moved to the UK at age 7, when his father was posted overseas. Small World!!!!!

He retired from playing in 2019 and took up coaching, before landing a job as Phase Development Coach with Forest Green Rovers in January 2022.

The next player on my list of rememberable players is Charles Adesola Oludare Oluwatosi Ademeno. He signed for Crawley from Southend United at the beginning of the 2009/2010 season, making 32 appearances and scoring a respectable total of eleven goals. He left at the end of the season to play for a bigger club, Grimsby Town, and must have thought he had done the right thing, when on the first day of the 2010/11 season Grimsby won one nil at the Broadfield. He didn't score however, in a game where Michel Kuipers was sent off. There were people doubting our credentials, which only goes to show that there is always hope.

The one game that I remember most featuring Charlie, was away to Grays Athletic. The supporters coach was held up in traffic and I just got into the ground to see him celebrating his second goal before notching his hat trick after just six minutes. Crawley, being Crawley, then contrived to let in two goals before half time but hung on for a three two win.

He went on to play for AFC Wimbledon, in their first year in the EFL, Eastbourne Borough, Salisbury City and Margate before retiring in 2014. He never repeated his goal scoring form that he enjoyed with Crawley Town.

Since the departure of Jon Paul Pittman, we have been blessed with an increasing number of players with a BAME background, most of whom have made significant contributions to Crawley Town such as Enzio Boudewijn, Bez Lubala and Paneutche Camara, but the three that I am going to conclude this chapter with, stand out I feel as being icons in our recent history.

The first two are Pablo Mills and Dean Howell. They both signed for us in the summer of 2010, although Pablo had previously been with us in 2007, on loan from Rotherham United. The reason for his loan was due to him reporting back for pre-season at the New York Stadium reputedly 3 stone overweight. Whilst with us that year he made 14 appearances and scored one goal before being recalled by Rotherham, where eventually he was made captain and at the end of the 2009/10 season, he featured in the League 2 play off final at Wembley on the losing side against Dagenham and Redbridge. Substituted in the 77th minute, he was released after the match and was snapped up by Steve Evans in his preparation for Project Promotion.

During the next two years at Broadfield Stadium, he made 53 appearances and scored five goals as centre back. In Project Promotion, two of the three goals he scored that year were winning goals, scored in the space of four days against Southport and Barrow. The other goal being in a five nil defeat of Hayes and Yeading.

He finished the season holding the conference pyramid above his head after being Man of the Match at Old Trafford and going on to win the Crawley Observer Player of the Year and being selected for the conference team of the year.

The following season he made fewer appearances, due to injury, but still managed two goals, one of them being against his former club, Rotherham United. His most memorable game that year though, must be the infamous Battle of Valley Parade. On 27 March 2012, he was involved in a post-match fight and was shown a red card along with four other players (one Crawley and three Bradford).[As a result, he was given a three-match ban as well as being stripped of his captaincy and fined two weeks' wages.

The match was the fourth game in a run of 10 unbeaten matches, which was much needed, as in the previous 7 games we had failed to win any and had slumped out of the promotion race. Incidentally, we had won against Bradford by two goals to one, our goals being scored by Gary Alexander and Leon Clarke.

Pablo wrote an extremely sincere letter of apology to the club, the fans and his family for his behaviour, and as everyone knows left us at the end of the season with another promotion for his c.v. and as a true Crawley Town legend.

Dean Howell, like Pablo Mills, signed for us in the summer of 2010 as part of Project Promotion and soon became a fans' favourite because of his ability to defend, attack and do almost anything that was asked of him.

He came to us as a free agent, after having been released by Aldershot, and, in the two seasons he was at Broadfield, played 72 games as well as making 16 substitute appearances. His only goal in the Conference season came in the penultimate game of the season, when he collected a cross field pass from Richard Brodie, waltzed past two Newport County defenders and hit an unstoppable shot from some 25 yards which almost took the net with it. Crawley held on from the 68th minute to gain revenge for the home defeat inflicted back in October 2010, the last time we had lost in the league. This marked the 29th game undefeated since that 2 – 3 loss, a run that was extended to 30 when we finished the season with a one all draw against York City at home.

He also scored, this time from a low driven free kick, against Dartford in the FA Trophy, to earn us a replay, which unfortunately we lost.

The following season in League 2, he continued to be a first team regular, playing 44 games in total across League and cups, and scored another three goals, all at home and all from distance. The unlucky opponents were Southend, Shrewsbury and Oxford United, defeated three nil, two one and four one respectively.

Dean's ability to get up and down the field with the utmost efficiency in defence and attack was what made him so popular, and if asked what enabled him to be so fit, he would no doubt tell you it was all down to his Vegan lifestyle. It was the loss of his grandmother that made him look at his lifestyle and when he noted that not eating dairy products improved his fitness, he decided to take his changes even further, giving up meat, fish and alcohol. In his own words he stated why.

"I ended up having my best years in football once I went plant-based, …...I stopped drinking alcohol. My lifestyle changed, so that collectively it would have made a bigger impact. I consume food for fuel, I've lost that emotional thing to it [meat]. I don't need to think or smell a burger and stuff like that to make me want to eat it. I just don't eat it, period."

From a personal point of view, I admire him for his stance, which has led him to start up his own business (Revolution Foods) and the memory that most sticks out in my mind is that famous moment when he found Sergio Torres from a corner at the southeastern part of the ground, which Sergio drove into the net to defeat Derby County and start Steve Evans dancing on the sidelines.

The best Crawley Town full back? Perhaps not. The best winger? Not sure. But, without a doubt the best wing back to play for the Red Devils ….......IMHO

The subject of the next few pages, and the last in the series about Crawley Town BAME players, is someone all our current set of supporters can relate to. It is, of course, Lewis Young. I am not going into the ins and outs of his departure from our club, as this book is not the platform for that discussion, but I will start with his dad who came over to this country from Jamaica with his parents. Luther Young was on his way to play in a trial match for QPR at the age of 16, when he was knocked off his bike by a bus. The knee injury he suffered curtailed any chance of a professional football career, although he did play in the FA Cup at non-league level.

Years later, after Luther married, he moved to Stevenage, where his family grew to include four sons, all with football aspirations of their own. Martin, the oldest, who six years ago was playing non-league football in Oxfordshire, was described by Lewis as "probably the most talented" of them all but then went on to state "his journey was cut short by choices he made when he was younger".

Ashley, now 37 and playing back at Aston Villa after an illustrious career, mainly at Manchester United and England, played in the same school team as one Lewis Hamilton, and both their pictures adorn the covered walkway at Stevenage railway station as prominent sons of the town.

Lewis Young's youngest brother, Kyle, was tipped to surpass even Ashley's talents, when excelling in Arsenal's youth academy, a hip deformity was eventually discovered at 19 after three years of misdiagnoses and examinations with various surgeons. Since then, he has had a hip replacement which has sadly curtailed his football career.

Lewis is recorded as having said this about Kyle when interviewed by the Sun newspaper back in 2017. "We had really high hopes that he would go on and achieve more than any of us. He's just finishing off a plumbing course so he should be a qualified plumber within the year. It's not something he wanted to do when he was younger but it's something he's enjoying now. He's still a big supporter on the sidelines when he can get to a game on a Saturday."

Now let's look at the life and career of Lewis himself.

Lewis was born in Stevenage in 1989 and attended St Vincent de Paul Primary and Nobel secondary school. Following in Ashley's footsteps, he joined Watford's academy in 2006 as he approached his 17th birthday. After two years at the academy, he signed on professional forms for the club and made two appearances for the club, one in a league cup victory over Bristol Rovers and one in a four two home defeat on Boxing Day against Bristol City, replacing another future Red Devil in Matt Sadler. Both of those first team appearances happened in his first season with the Hornets and towards the end of his second year he was loaned out to Hereford United on a one-month loan deal, and on 20 March 2010 he made his debut in a 2–0 victory over Bradford City, playing the full 90 minutes.

In the next four seasons Lewis gained experience at Burton Albion, Forest Green Rovers, Northampton, Yeovil, Aldershot and Bury before signing for us at the beginning of the 2014/15 season under the then Crawley Town manager, John Gregory.

In his first season with us, he either played on the right side of midfield or, on occasions, just behind Izale Mcleod up front. He actually scored four goals for us that season, all in the Sussex Senior Cup, including a hat trick against St Francis Rangers in a home game played at Oakwood in front of just 203 supporters in a six two "home" victory, and our solitary goal in the next round at Whitehawk in an ignominious six one defeat to a team which, I seem to recall, included a certain Argentinian legend called Sergio Torres.

His first season with Crawley ended in relegation, but really shouldn't have with three games left. In the first of those games, all featuring Lewis Young, we beat Notts County by two goals to nil, and changed places with them, getting ourselves out of the bottom four and three points clear of the drop. The next two games were heartbreaking, to say the least, as, leading three two away to Peterborough in the 87th minute, we then conceded twice in the last three minutes to drop us back into the bottom four. Worst of all, Michael Bostwick, an ex-red himself, scored one of those goals.

The last day of the season saw us facing Coventry City at home just two points behind them but with a much inferior goal difference. If we had won we would have been saved, however, it wasn't to be, although at one point of the game we did lead through Matthias Pogba but two late goals from Coventry sent us down, the last being scored by James Maddison in the 90th minute. A win was the only thing that could have saved us and Colchester United leap frogged us from 48 points to 51 , sending us, Notts County, Leyton Orient and Yeovil down to League 2. All this happening under the tutilage of Dean Saunders, who had taken over from John Gregory at Christmas, due to John needing heart surgery.

The next season , back in League 2, saw Lewis become a regular in the side making 38 league appearances including nine as substitute. The season for the team as a whole was one of struggle, In the league we finished on 47 points and didn't collect any points in the last eight games. Our cup fortunes were no better, going out of all but one at the first attempt. Luckily, in the league, there were four teams worse than us with Dagenham & Redbridge and York City finishing on just 34 pointsand dropping into the National League. Mark Yates, our manager at the time , left at the end of the season to be replaced by Dermot Drummy, Lewis' fifth manager in just two short years. Sounds familiar, doesn't it.

Dermot Drummy lasted nearly the whole season before Matt Harrold took over for the last game as caretaker. Lewis played forty-two games in that season which saw us finish 19th on 51 points, gaining just one win in the last fourteen matches. Another season which promised so much but ended with us just escaping relegation, and ultimately, rather sadly, lead to the loss of one of the nicest men in football.

Away from football Lewis married Joy, his partner, and now, in 2023, has three children. His brother-in-law is Stevenage forward Luke Norris, but as yet, I do not think they have played professionally together.

I asked whether he had come across any racial barriers in his footballing career or in life in general, without going into any specifics. His response was that he had heard racist chants directed at him and other players, and decided to rise above them on the field by attempting to show it didn't bother him. He did say he accepts people shouting about his perceived mistakes but does not see why his colour is a factor. His one regret must be the comments made to Joy by people in general asking why she has chosen to be with him. These encounters have happened whilst they have been out for dinner and are too graphic to be quoted here.

The next season started with the appointment of ex Liverpool and Leeds United star, Harry Kewell, as our manager and saw Lewis maintain his almost 100% appearance record, which was made even more impressive when, on the 3rd of February 2018, he was played in by Jimmy Smith to score a 93rd minute winner against

Chesterfield away. I am pretty sure John Barnett was commentating that day and came out with the unforgettable line "Look at his face, just look at his face!!!!" as Lewis went on an excited run towards the away support with all the team following behind.

One match later, after beating Grimsby three goals to nil, Crawley stood in 10th place in the league, just four points off the playoff positions on forty-eight points. However, despite Lewis scoring another two goals, against Cheltenham and Coventry, both in home defeats, the team could not maintain their impressive form. This saw the Red Devils pick up just 11 points out of a possible 42 finishing in 14th place on 59 points.

Season 2018/19 saw, after just seven games, Harry Kewell leave the club for a much "bigger" club in Notts County, only to part company with them halfway through the season which ended in them being relegated. Lewis made another 33 appearances scoring yet another goal, this time earning us a point against Macclesfield Town at the Broadfield. Philipe Morais and Jimmy Smith acted as caretakers for Lincoln City away before Gabrielle Cioffi and Edu Rubio were appointed Manager and assistant for the rest of the season.

Season 2019/20 saw Lewis play just 15 league games and score his last Crawley Town goal, before a spinal injury put an end to his playing career, his last game being away to Grimsby, where coincidentally Jake Hessenthaler scored for the Lincolnshire side in the 2nd minute and Ashley Nadesan earned us a point with a 37th Minute equaliser.

Two games before that was when he scored that last goal, away at Boundary Park, when in the 17th minute he danced his way infield unchallenged from the right flank, slotting a neat left-footed shot home to put the reds one up in a game we eventually lost two one. Going another two games back that season saw the first game with John Yems in charge after the sacking of Gaby Cioffi just a few days earlier. The game was the New Town Derby away at Stevenage, which ended in a nil nil draw spoilt by the behaviour of some of our support. Thankfully right-minded

Crawley supporters managed to calm everyone down, but it must be said it left a bad taste in the mouth for all those who care about the image of our club.

The season, three months later, prematurely came to an end with the onset of the covid pandemic and the 2020/21 season saw Lewis Young as part of the coaching set up under John Yems and Lee Bradbury. A season mostly played in front of no fans saw a mid-table finish and arguably the best result in our history against Leeds United.

Fast forward on another year and just at the time Wagmi were buying the club from Ziya Eren, Crawley Town parted company with John Yems, which led to Lewis Young taking over as caretaker manager for the last three games. His record was lost two, drawn one which unsurprisingly saw the appointment of Kevin Betsy as first team coach for the 2022/23 season. Despite putting Fulham out of the League Cup our very poor league form led to Betsy's departure in October, which gave Lewis his second opportunity to be in charge. The players responded to him and in his time at the top we won three, drew three and lost just one of our league games and put on a good performance away to Burnley in the League Cup. We all know he didn't get the job permanently, with opinions split as to whether he warranted it or not, but I do know, in having the privilege to interview him, that he is an honest and thoroughly decent man who deserves to succeed in whatever he chooses to do.

When I asked him who his role models were, he put his mum and dad ahead of Lilian Thuram and Paul Parker. A true measure of the man.

Lewis Young, six seasons playing for Crawley Town, 213 games played, and five league goals scored, two spells as gaffer covering 10 league games, winning three, drawing four and losing three.

Chapter Five

"Who really owns a football club?"

As most Crawley Town fans will know, most of this book has been published, on an almost weekly basis, in the Crawley Observer and the Crawley Town matchday programmes under the title Stagni Ollam Et Superbus. This chapter is entitled "Who really owns a football club?", and this is what I told Mark Dunford (Crawley Observer) it would be about when I submitted him the Lewis Young section. I then explained to him, at the Crawley Town Supporters Alliance AGM, on the 2nd of February 2023, that it wasn't going to be an exclusive about Preston Johnson or Wagmi United, but rather how the ownership model had changed over the years, especially with regards to Crawley FC and Crawley Town FC.

In the beginning, God created Crawley FC! Well, almost. Go back to the beginning if you don't believe me. The Rectory for St John the Baptist Church in Crawley, was, in the 1890s, at the end of a fairly long, and no doubt dusty lane, which started where the Boulevard now starts, in between the Old Punch Bowl and the Crawley Museum, or the Tree as it was then called.

The House itself stood roughly where the Platform apartments are now, or for those of older years, where Woodall Duckham, Babcocks and Doosan had their offices. Behind the rectory was Rectory field where after church Sunday schools were held, featuring athletic pursuits such as football and cricket. It could be said that this was where our club was born, as borne out by the earlier chapters about Bill Denman.

In those days, the club was not owned as such, but run by a committee including local businessmen, farmers, doctors, and other such people. The players would have been drawn from the local farms, merchants and railway workers and would not have been paid but would have more likely paid a subscription.

Farmers, such as Mr. Stone, would have provided the "meadow" to play on and would also, no doubt, have tried to make it as playable as possible.

Ownership was thus more a community thing, and the committee ruled the roost.

This was certainly the case at our level, right up until the end of the Second World War, and indeed there probably wasn't the need for extra finance to come into the club until we turned semiprofessional in 1962. The benefactors, which up to then were Vice-Presidents, leaving the everyday running of the club to a committee, started to be known as Directors who sat on a board with a committee still underneath them. Directors gave their money; the committee gave their time and labour.

From my point of view, it was also about this time that supporters started to become a real entity, providing gate money, supporting the team and sadly becoming a little divorced from the actual running of the club.

As time progressed, the committee morphed into the non-playing staff of the club, such as ground staff, catering staff, administration staff etc.etc, and we find ourselves where we were back in 2004 when the players became fully professional. Meanwhile, the size of support had grown as had players wages and fans expectations.

Professional Players, managers and background staff, which just leaves the supporters who give their all, in time and money, with just a hope that they will be rewarded by a good league finish or a run in a cup. Since the 1960s we have experienced both the highs and lows of supporting a football club, five promotions including two championships, numerous league and Sussex cups to our credit and some fantastic FA and League Cup runs, set against two relegations and numerous barren years in the FA Cup. And that is just on the playing side. We have had a succession of owners, some good, some not so and, indeed, some who were outright catastrophic. Today's owners should not yet receive the final judgement, and one can only hope that by the time you read this, in book form, we are looking forward to our 13th year in League football.

During all that time our support has fluctuated like our performances on the pitch and has been represented for the most part by the Supporters Club and in later years by the CTSA formerly known as the Devil's Trust. With some owners the relationship between the Supporters Organisations has been fruitful, but with some it bordered on toxic.

I don't believe it's just a coincidence that our poorest times, in terms of finances, have been since we turned fully professional in 2004. Players who once had careers outside football and thought of football as providing pocket money were replaced, if only in mentality, by players who needed to draw a living wage from the game they should all love. Supporters, because of this, expected more of the men who wore the red of Crawley Town.

Supporters Organisations, not just in Crawley but, all over the UK are now trying to get back to the times when supporters were really involved in their club, not just in having a say but also in having a share in the club they support which brings us to whether it is right to say "My" or "our" club when we talk about them.

For me and my family it will always be my and our club, whether we have a financial stake in it or not. It is mine and ours for the times we have stood in the cold to watch them; for the times we have jumped in the air when we have won in the dying minutes; for the despair we have felt when we have been on the opposing end of such an experience; for the wonderful days out at places such as Tonbridge, Welling, Tamworth, Accrington, Manchester and Hull.....and even Burnley;* for the sharing of defeats, even when it meant relegation. All these instances, and similar, make real supporters, not just in Crawley but no doubt for clubs up and down the country.

Crawley Town is MY club, OUR club and that should never be forgotten, although I, and I believe most other supporters, am grateful to those people with the money who, in Dictionary terms, really do own the club.

Now to get that Euromillions Lottery ticket!!!

* Were you there at Hartlepool, I'm glad to say I was, as that game should now be etched into every Reds fan's memory banks. It was the day we stood tall and survived.

Please read on for coverage of our club from September 2021 upto the end of the 2022/23 season, not in match reports but in my weekly "Thoughts of a life-long fan" as published in the Crawley Observer.

Part Two: Photo Gallery

Crawley FC 1890 with Bill Denman (Age 12) first left middle row
Credit: Nadine Hygate "Crawley revisited"

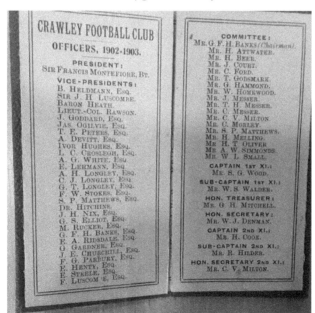

Crawley FC 1902-03 Club Directory

The 1903 winning Crawley FC team with the Mid-Sussex Football League Challenge Shield

ROLL OF HONOUR

GORING A.	JOHNSON W.
GORRINGE E.	JOHNSTONE R.J.E.
GRAVELY C.	JORDON L.G.
HAWKINS G.K.	KERREY E.J.
HARDING F.A.	KILLICK F.
HEATHER A.	KILLICK J.
HEDGER F.	KILLICK S.
HERITAGE J.	KING C.
HILDER R.	KNOWLES H.
HILTON F.	LAKER A.
HOLDER J.	LAW S.
HOLTON R.H.	LILLYWHITE W.
HOY J.	LINFIELD E.
HUMPHREY J.	LUCAS D.L.
HUMPHREY M.J.	MARTIN H.G.
HYGATE H.P.	MITCHELL C.K.
IZARD J.W.	MOORE R.J.
JOHNSON J.	MOSSE P.G.
JOHNSON R.J.	

The Crawley Memorial Garden Gates commemorating the service given by Crawley men, including James and William Johnson.

Bill Denman in his First World War uniform.

*Mr W J Denman JP, Chair of Crawley FC, Crawley CC
and the Bonfire Society 1932*

Bill and Helen's resting place, St John the Baptist, Crawley.

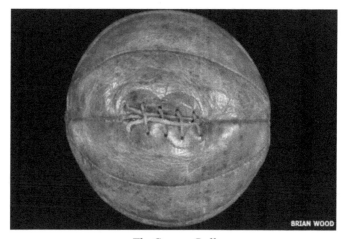

The Somme Ball

Rector's Chair

The Barrett-Lennard family window

George Banks through the ages, 30, 32 and 56

Stan in action in the Millwall Shield final, 1938

Stan and Alma

*Stan next to Ted Ditchburn, with Alf Ramsey on his far right
and Bill Nicholson, far left one row down*

Gloves? Don't be silly!!

Ray Carter 1963

1968-69 Promotion winners, Back: Goodgame, Leedham, Leck,
Maggs, Blaber, Cockell, McMullen, March
Front: Basey, Haining, Bragg, Standing, Tharme.

John Leedham out jumping three Chelmsford City players in the Cup.

Stan, making a deal or arranging a fixture

Stan in his Upjohn European Champions blazer
(Can you spot Steve Preest, Walking footballers?)

Stan, on the left with the 83/84 promotion side.
Can you name them all?

Programme from 11 days after his passing.
We lost, but went on to win the treble that year, League,
League Cup and the equivalent of the
Southern League Charity Shield.
No one would have been happier than Stan

The Main stand at Ashford Town (Middlesex) built in 1998,
paid for by Bully's transfer to Wycombe

Dannie in his early days at Adams Park

The winning goal against Leicester City as seen by Dannie,
just after he has crossed the ball to Bates, who heads it back
for Essandoh to score his one and only goal for Wycombe

Matt Tubbs scoring the winner at Torquay
after receiving a dream Bulman pass

Dannie, leading the singing the day we won the Conference title

Legends and friends in the wrong-coloured shirts

Captain Courageous credit Sussex Express

"Vic Marley was the first face I saw when coming through the door, what a lovely genuine man, Legend." Dannie Bulman

John Hollins

Scott Neilson secures promotion to League 1

Gums, Mr Evans?

Trevor Smith, far right, with 1980/81 team at Haywards Heath

● Crawley Town Reserves pictured before the kick off against Pagham at Town Mead on Saturday,

SMITH B.TCHLEY, G COLLYER, J ETHERIDGE, BOLLVER, J COCK, A SIMMONS
K REGO, D HAINING, J LINCOLN, B MORGAN, T STILWELL, B GODDARD

Keith Rego, front left, next to Dave Haining

Keith Rego circa 2022

Back Row: Markham, McMillan, Bragg, Breach, De Souza, Keeping,
Harriott, Roberts, Haining, Maggs
Front Row: Burtenshaw, Page, Wallace, Grabban, Cant, Gregory
on the billiard table surface that was Town Meadow

Ben Abbey

Francis Vines

Gavin Holigan
Footballer, turned Musician

Nigel and Ann Brake

JP Pittman as he is now

Charlie Ademeno against our friends from ...Wimbledon

Pablo Mills

Deano taking care of Chicarito

Ashley, Lewis, Kyle and Martin Young

Lewis Young after scoring in the 93rd minute at Chesterfield
"Look at his face, just look at his face!!!!"

Lewis Young 2021

Eric Strange, at his last Crawley Town game

Part Three
Thoughts of a life-long fan

Chapter One

2021/2022

Ladies and Gentlemen, girls and boys, before you get into my thoughts of the two seasons covered in this book, here are the league results for 2021/2022 for you to review and remember what you were doing for each game. The results are shown with the Crawley Town score first, whether at home or away, followed by the attendance and the position in the league at full time.

7 / 8/ 2021   Hartlepool United   Away 0–1 5,184 20th

17 /8/2021   Salford City   Home 2–1 2167 13th
Nadesan 38', Hessenthaler 75'

21 /8/ 2021   Forest Green Rovers   Away 3–6 1922 19th
Hessenthaler 14', 30', Appiah 86'

28 /8/ 2021   Northampton Town   Home 0–0 2,254 20th

4 /9/ 2021   Bristol Rovers   Away 0–1 6,513 22nd

11 /9/ 2021   Carlisle United   Home 2–1 2151 19th
Nichols 32', Tsaroulla 90'

18 /9/2021   Colchester United   Away 1–0 2640 14th
Payne 22'

21 /9/ 2021   Harrogate Town   Home 2–2 1791 12th
Lynch 42', Ashford 45+1'

25 /9/ 2021   Bradford City   Home 2–1 2435 8th
Ferry 39', Tsaroulla 73'

Date	Opponent		Venue	Result	Att.	Pos.
2 /10/ 2021	Tranmere Rovers Appiah 64'		Away	1–2	6046	14th
9/10/ 2021	Rochdale Appiah 14'		Away	1–0	2268	9th
16 /10/2021	Sutton United		Home	0–1	3,572	12th
19 /10/ 2021	Exeter City Appiah 31'		Home	1–3	1960	14th
23 /10/ 2021	Scunthorpe United Appiah 73'		Away	1-2	2112	16th
30 /10/ 2021	Port Vale Appiah 44'		Home	1–4	2234	18th
20 /11/ 2021	Barrow Tilley 56'		Away	1–0	3429	18th
23 /11/ 2021	Newport County Appiah 55'		Home	1–1	1483	19th
27 /11/ 2021	Mansfield Town Tilley 48'		Home	1–2	1824	18th
7 /12/ 2021	Walsall Nichols 45+1'		Away	1-1	3609	18th
11 /12/ 2021	Leyton Orient Francomb 32', Appiah 66'		Away	2-1	5142	16th
1 /1/2022	Colchester United Nadesan (2) 15', 55', Lynch 37'		Home	3–1	2022	14th
8 /1/ 2022	Northampton Town Nichols 41'		Away	1–0	4714	11th
15/1/ 2022	Carlisle United Nadesan 25'		Away	1–1	4350	11th

18 /1/ 2022	Stevenage Nichols 45+1'	Away	1–2	1942	12th
22 /1/ 2022	Tranmere Rovers	Home	0–1		14th
29 /1/2022	Bradford City Nichols 71', Craig 90+5'	Away	2–1	14263	13th
1 /2/ 2022	Swindon Town Powell 41' (pen.)	Away	1–1	7306	14th
5/2/ 2022	Stevenage Nichols (2) 34', 46'	Home	2–2	2214	14th
8 /2/ 2022	Harrogate Town Oteh 48', Tsaroulla 79', Nichols 84'	Away	3–1	1785	12th
12 /2/ 2022	Hartlepool United	Home	0–1	2,228	12th
26 /2 2022	Forest Green Rovers Nadesan 24', Tunnicliffe 32'	Home	2–1	2086	13th
1 /3/ 2022	Oldham Athletic Nadesan (2) 58', 61'	Home	2–2		12th
5/3/2022	Scunthorpe United	Home	0–0	2144	13th
8 /3/2022	Bristol Rovers Hessenthaler 69'	Home	1–2	2223	13th
12 /3/2022	Port Vale Smith 9' (o.g.)	Away	1–4	5131	13th
15 /3/ 2022	Exeter City Appiah 45+6'	Away	1–2	4042	15th
19 /3/ 2022	Swindon Town Appiah 29', Nichols 72', Hutchinson 90+1'	Home	3–1	2977	13th
26/3/ 2022	Rochdale Nadesan 18'	Home	1–0	2164	12th
29 /3/ 2022	Salford City Nichols 82'	Away	1-2	1290	13th

85

9 /4/ 2022	Barrow Appiah 57'	Home 1–0 2081 12th
15/4/ 2022	Newport County Nadesan 15', Francillette 21'	Away 2–1 5137 12th
18/4/ 2022	Walsall Hutchinson 69'	Home 1-0 2258 12th
23/4/ 2022	Mansfield Town	Away 0–2 5022 12th
27 /4/2022	Sutton United	Away 0–3 3,109 12th
30 /4/2022	Leyton Orient	Home 0–2 3372 12th
7 May 2022	Oldham Athletic Francomb 39', Tilley 44', Oteh 69'	Away 3–3 4591 12th

Tuesday 31st August 2021 is the last day to be featured in "Noli Semper Cedere" and I was hoping for us to be top of the League, still to be in the League Cup and at least to have taken Charlton Athletic to a bonus point penalty shootout.

Well, that didn't go to plan, did it? Good job I had clean pants on though. To explain, this evening marked my first trip with G&H and probably my last. Not because of them, as their demeanour throughout was first class, but because of what happened to me on the relatively short trip to south east London. The coach was almost full and Chris Hewlett, the club safety officer, was sitting next to me as we headed north. As we approached the A2 I started to sweat profusely and became nauseous, and as a precaution I asked Chris if he could get me a sick bag, which thankfully, Alain Harper provided just in time before I started to vomit. Chris then phoned through to his counterpart at the Valley, and when we arrived, we were met by a St John's Ambulance team, who wheelchaired me into the stadium to their impressive sick bay area. The route taken took us past the away dressing room and a bemused looking Lewis Young, as he saw me in my vomit-stained clothing. (Yes, the bag was as leaky as our defence was about to become). After a thorough check over by Millwall supporting medical personnel, including an ECG, I was passed fit to go into the stadium, knowing that after just twenty minutes we were already three down because of the cheers we had heard in the bowels of the stadium's sick bay. I sat next to Chris for the duration of the game, not really there in my head, and not really bothered about the result. Charlton were a faster side than us on the day and every shot they took seemed to fly in, but even at four nil when Ashley Nadesan was bundled over in the box and Quesi Appiah scored from the resultant penalty, the boy in me thought "one more lads, make them nervous", but it wasn't to be and the Addicks added another two to make it six one and complete our defeat. Were the fans who travelled down hearted? No, they weren't, although one of them may regret his pitch incursion adventure, as they sang throughout and exchanged light hearted banter with the Charlton librarians. Dreading the journey home, I did manage to make it back to Crawley, vomit free, where I was well looked after by my daughter and wife. Many people will know, that in the past, Alain and I have had our disagreements about supporter representation and all that involves, but I have always appreciated the work he does to support the team we all love and cannot thank him enough for the way he and Chris Hewlett dealt with me last night.

When I watched John Yems' post-match interview I found myself trying to read between the lines. Did his reference to Harry Ransom, needing to go to Lourdes to get some energy, indicate that perhaps he had suffered from Covid, and is maybe still suffering from its after effects or even long covid? Not sure if I have remembered his words correctly, but he also alluded to "being allowed to do what I want to do". Only time will tell, I guess, what that is, but I do feel we have the right players, when fit, to get us up the league and I will still feel the same way if we have, by the time you read this, lost against a falsely positioned Bristol Rovers. They have added several experienced players in the transfer window, which I feel may be our Achilles heel at the moment, in that several of our experienced players, such as Nico, Tunni, Reece and now Dallo are being sorely missed at the moment. I welcome the arrival of Amrit, but he is only 21, and therefore one can only hope that he hits the ground running and that his enthusiasm and energy makes up for his youthful inexperience. Of course, we might have beaten Bristol and in that case the world will seem a whole light brighter.

15th September 2021

Oh, what a goal,

Mid-September back in '21,

We couldn't believe what he had done

As we remember, what a goal

Oh, what a win,

You know, we thought we had drawn the game

But now he belongs in the hall of fame

What a player, what a win

Oh, I, I got a funny feeling

When he shot, on the run.

And then the whistle blew

Game over, we had won

Oh, what a team!!!!

Ok, I'll get my coat and stick to my day job, only I haven't got one. A job that is. Seriously though, what a perfect example of Noli Semper Cedere (Never Ever Give Up), I only hope Jermaine Beckford was watching. If you don't get the meaning of that slightly sarcastic comment, something which I was told never to use as a teacher so I'm making up for it now, have a look back at his comments after we had demolished his beloved Leeds United. Nick Tsaroulla, what a player! Does he only score goals of the season?

The whole day for me was perfect, starting with the pre-match drink in Redz, the coming together of friends, old and new, through the drawing of September's Reds rollover by John "Yemsy" Yems and Dannie "the legend" Bulman, ably assisted by young Elliot Jordan and finally concluding with that stunning 90th minute winner

The game itself was what football at our level is all about, end to end stuff with chances in both penalty areas providing us with three goals, two for us and one for them, but most importantly with the three points. There were stars all over the pitch, but three stood out for me in being the reason for us getting the result. The first was new signing, Joel Lynch, who despite his booking proved to be an experienced commanding presence at the back alongside Tom Dallison. The second was Tom Nichols, who proved yet again what an instinctive, hardworking player he is and put us into the lead for the first time this season, and of course, the third was young Nick Tsaroulla, who, despite missing a tackle on half way which led to their equaliser , never gave up and hit the sweetest of volleys to send the Crawley faithful into a state of wonderful delirium.

Our home form is great, with two wins and a draw against three of the fancied teams, but now is the time to get the away form going as we travel the relatively short distance to deepest Essex. There will be a good reds presence at Colchester, providing of course everyone has managed to pass the entrance exam for buying a ticket, with many travelling by car, coach and train. I am positive it will be a good day out whatever the outcome, but it would be even better if we were to come home with all three points. Let's hope the only problems John and Lee have to face, before next Saturday, are who to leave out of the match day squad because they are all fit and available.

Away from the on-pitch stuff, I am pleased to announce that Noli Semper Cedere is now at the publishers and should be available in October, with the official launch scheduled to take place at the Port Vale home game on the 30th. Typically, as soon as I had submitted the draft copy, I discovered some more exciting information about the origins of our club which left me in a bit of a quandary. Do I rewrite the draft or write a third book? After much careful thought, I have decided to do the latter and, thanks to Ivan Noel, I already have the title, "Stagni Ollam et Superbus". I'll leave the translation to you.!!

22nd September 2021

Stacey Solomon, Ollie Murs, Gemma Collins, Rylan Clarke-Neil, Denise Van Outen, Alastair Cooke, Fathima Whitbread, we have beaten them all, we have beaten them all. Dermot O'Leary can you hear me? Dermot O'Leary.....your boys took a hell of a beating! Your boys took a hell of a beating! THE ONLY WAY IS SUSSEX.

Paraphrasing Bjorge Lillelien there, with his infamous tirade that he gave after Norway had beaten the Three Lions back in 1981 on the 9th September, but I'm jumping the gun abit as the story of a wonderful day started some 10 hours earlier. Woke up, got out of bed, dragged a comb across my head. Found My way downstairs, ate my overnight oats and drank a cup, made sure I had my printed-out ticket to get me into the Colchester Stadium and made Three Bridges Station in 45 minutes, which isn't that bad for a 70-year-old Parkinson's sufferer with a stick

At the station I met Matt Jenkins, Steve Herbert and Dan Hyre and soon we were on the 10.10 to Farringdon teaming up with fellow reds Keith Miller and Paul Wakeford. The journey to London, on the advice of our Herbert's tours rep, was curtailed at London Bridge and we took to the tube exiting at Moorgate for the short walk to Liverpool Street station where we met six more Reds; Dame Carol Bates, Andy Tester, Marilyn Loughton, Dan Palmer, Rob Beeching and Dan Jones. The last of those, Dan Jones, deserves a special mention. He is from Liverpool, studying politics and economics at Leeds University, and he became a real red after the Old Trafford game in 2011, when just a boy. He had already seen us play at Hartlepool, and travelled down to London yesterday to join with us for the trip to Camulodunum where venimus, vidimus, vicimus, so to speak.

When we finally got to the stadium, after a lunch time drink or two, we joined another 161 Crawley Town supporters, including my daughter Vicky, her husband Nick and Beth and Oliver, my grandchildren, and settled down for what turned out to be a very memorable match. Before the game, however, a few words were politely exchanged with the stewards and the catering staff about Colchester's overzealous ticketing system which was totally negated by their "sit where you like" welcome, and also about the shortage of sustenance provided for a contingent that they knew the numbers of in advance.

On to the game, and understandably an unchanged side from that which defeated Carlisle last Saturday and from the outset it was clear we were in for a good afternoon. A resolute back four, and the rejuvenated Glen Morris, provided the platform from which our midfield and forwards could advance on the Colchester goal and after a couple of thwarted chances the breakthrough came in the 22nd minute, when Tomm Dallison found Will Ferry on the right, who beat the full back and superbly laid the ball into the path of Jack Payne who stroked it into the net.

The supporters were in good voice throughout and Colchester never really looked like pegging us back. Indeed, with a little bit of luck and a following wind, we really should have scored at least two more which would have been a fairer reflection of the way we had played. Game over, I chose to get a lift back to Crawley with my family, rather than go for more beer with the lads, I know, I'm getting old, and was pleasantly surprised to experience Colchester fans applauding us in the car park, whether it be for our support or style of play, or both.

The morning after, the pragmatist in me realises that this result will amount to nothing unless we get something from the next two home games against Harrogate and Bradford City. Last season we played two home games in a row on four occasions. On two of those occasions, we lost both home games, whilst on the other two we won both. If you want an omen though, the only time those two home games followed an away victory came in March after our one nil win at Tranmere, and we went on to beat Salford and Mansfield by the same score in the following week.

29th September 2021

If, in a few weeks, when you're watching "Would I lie to you?", and comedian Maisie Adam claims to have been in the home end at the Crawley Town v Harrogate game, she will be telling the truth. Born in Pannal, close to Harrogate, she was spotted, hood up, just as Sam Ashford put the Red Devils into the lead on the stroke of half time. At least she saw both the Crawley goals, which is more than can be said for some of our own supporters who had evacuated to the bar when we were one nil down.

The turnaround in the game caught everybody by surprise, with the goals by Joel Lynch and Sam Ashford top trumping the Sulphurites' goal, scored by Armstrong in our seemingly ubiquitous "haven't woken up" phase at the beginning of the game. For me though, the game pivoted back into the away side's favour because of two incidents. The first, being when the revelation that is Joel Lynch overstretched in front of Ross and Tracey Thornton on the south west terrace, and the second being Nadders' moment of naivety in the second half. The injury to Lynch leaves us with just one fit centre back at the moment and we can only hope that one of them has recovered sufficiently enough so as not to hinder our progress up the league. Injuries happen and have to be dealt with, but to lose Nadders for three games for what was not a head butt, but just a head push, was avoidable. It was avoidable in that Ashley should never have let himself be goaded into that situation. Their number 20 used his head, excuse the pun, by backing away, which is exactly what Nadders didn't do. Personally, I think both players should have received the same card, be that yellow or red, but the whole irony of the situation is that the referee that gave the red card, Darren

Drysdale, was himself suspended for four weeks for a similar incident, when he allegedly squared up to Ipswich's Alan Judge when they were playing Northampton. Sounds like a load of old cobblers to me, but it does mean that one of our players, who reputedly "couldn't tackle a fish supper" will now be out for three games on top of our lengthy injury list. Good job he's not a centre back!!

The optimist in me hopes for better, more even-handed refereeing this afternoon against Bradford City.

And that is exactly what we got. Yes, the referee made some "errors", but they weren't costly to either side and the crowd of just over 2400 were treated to a game and a win for the Red Devils that moves us up to 8th in the table. The goals came from Will Ferry in the 39th minute, scoring his first in senior football, and the second came in the 73rd minute when Nick Tsaroulla slotted home from the edge of the box, thanks to an assist from yours truly, who, when he received the ball, shouted out "come on Nick, pretend they're Leeds". He did just that and, despite a late goal from the Bantams, the win was achieved. The centre back problem was eased by the return of Ludwig Francilette, who paired up well with Tom Dallison in the heart of the defense, and all in all it was a sound performance which extends our unbeaten home run to five games and stretches our run in all games to four. With two away games to come before we return to the People's Pension stadium, it was important to build upon the result at Colchester, and that's exactly what we have done. Tranmere and Rochdale are up next away, before we meet our closest geographical opponents in Sutton United. It would be great to see a near full house for that game, so why not try and entice a couple of extra people each to attend. You never know they might enjoy it.

On the book front, Noli Semper Cedere is almost published. The official launch date, for those people who have so generously backed the project, is scheduled for the Port Vale home game on Saturday 30th October.

6th October 2021

Before we talk about Tranmere. I want to mention fate, destiny, coincidence, God's divine plan or whatever you believe in with respect to Crawley Town FC.

If it hadn't been for some lads back in 1890 getting together to play football friendlies under the banner of Crawley FC, we might not have the same club we have today. Indeed, we might not have a club at all, whereas we might have been Premier league champions. Such is the nature of our existence. Personally, I'm glad it happened the way it did, with the local rector introducing the local youngsters to the beautiful game, and some of them at the young age of twelve forming the basis of the club that we all support today. The story of key people in the life of Crawley Town FC is one of emotion, tragedy, war, peace and above all else, a desire to Never Give Up.

This will be the premise of the third book in the CTFC saga, and, thanks to Ivan Noel, we already have its title. "Stagni Ollam Et Superbus" which translated is "Tinpot and proud". The book will tell the stories of the men and women who have made our club what it is today. I'm glad we have not had it all our own way through the years, because our status in the football hierarchy has mostly been achieved through hard work, tinged at times with hardship but also illuminated by some precious magic moments. I'm trying to say that the glorious moments, such as; Dartford at home 1969. Welling away 2004, Old Trafford and Tamworth 2011, Hull City and Accrington 2012, Stoke City 2019 and Leeds United this year, are all the more treasured because of the bad years along the way. Supporting Crawley Town, for me, compares to following England, but what better way is there of developing true character? Win, Lose or Draw, forever Red.

Which brings us to Tranmere (written in real time). How many centre halves do you need in a squad? At least seven, is the answer you're looking for. Yet another injury, this time to Ludwig Francilette with a head injury. I have the feeling that we need to score first at Prenton Park, with them having conceded only three goals so far, but unfortunately the Birkenhead side draw first blood on twenty-eight minutes with a close-range header from one of their centre backs Peter Clarke. Five minutes earlier though, Sam Ashford had hit the bar with a shot that according to the Tranmere commentators had their keeper beaten all ends up. No away commentary available for this game but, I have to say, the Tranmere lads are more than fair in their comments about our play, eulogising about an effort from Nick Tsaroulla early in the second half. Oh, my word, Tranmere have just conceded their fourth goal of the season and it has to go down to an astute substitution, with Kwesi Appiah replacing Archie Davies with half an hour to go. Sam Ashford seeing his shot saved by the Tranmere keeper but only to the feet of Kwesi who has made me feel a lot Appiah. Settle for the point or go for the win? Neither it seems, as Clarke scores his second with eleven minutes to go after Glenn has made a save and on comes Marshall for Ashford to try and rescue the point. I absolutely hate not being there, just listening on Ifollow, as you feel absolutely powerless, which is irrational, I know. As we enter added on time, and five extra minutes, we are giving it a go but all to no avail and we drop to fourteenth in the league. Tranmere go up to ninth but their commentators say they are as good as in 6th place, which means, on that logic, we are as good as in 11th. Well, I've now got to get back to my wife after a nervous afternoon following the Red Devils, which thankfully only involves taking twelve short steps downstairs. I know the travelling support will be feeling gutted, as they travel home, whether it be to Crawley or to one of our northern exiles' abodes, but we are just one point from the playoffs and a full seven from relegation. Watch out Rochdale!!!!

13th October 2021

I was dreading Saturday's game at Rochdale, not because I didn't think we had it in our capabilities to win, but because of the "old player coming back to haunt you" conundrum. In this case, not even an old player, as he was only twelve or thirteen when he was in our academy, just as it folded under an old regime. The player concerned is Danny Cashman, who is on loan at Rochdale from Coventry City, but he is a Crawley boy, who was taken up by the Seagulls after the closure of the academy at Broadfield, who is now making a career for himself in the beautiful game. An extremely personable young man, who was involved in a film made for Southern Water by the Crawley Town Community Foundation back when I was involved behind the scenes. Luckily, he only came on for about 30 minutes and only really threatened once, when Tony Craig took one for the team and stopped him in his tracks. Watching the game at home, thanks to the international weekend, I thought we fully deserved the win and really should have won by more. The inclusion of Appiah and Bansal-McNulty proved to be the catalyst for the performance, which, for once, earned its justifiable reward. Scoring through Kwesi Appiah early on there were only a few moments of worry after that and the delight shown by the Crawley fans was there for all to see. At one point in the afternoon, we were up to seventh and in the play-off places, but late winners for Sutton United and Hartlepool saw us having to settle for 9th place, but level on points with the teams above us. Next weekend, the A217 derby, against Sutton United, should see a large crowd at the People's pension stadium and it promises to be a humdinger of a game, with three ex Reds in their side in Rob Milsom, Louis John and Enzio Boldewijn, especially after they came back from two nil down to win four three in injury time against Port Vale. A win for the red devils will see us leap frog them in the league and will almost certainly put us into the play-off positions, albeit with only a quarter of the season played. However, when you consider the players missing from our team through injury it is nothing short of a miracle that we are so highly placed. Well done to the management and the players for putting us in such a strong position, as surely, we can only get stronger as the injured players return.

Next Saturday will also see supporters from both clubs competing against each other, prior to the big match, in a game of "while the cat's away" which involves trying to aim a ball through a hole as many times as you can within a certain amount of time. Pre or post drinks is surely the question which will determine the winners. The CTSA will also be holding this month's draw of the Reds Rollover with a first prize of £63, a second of £31.50, a third prize of two complimentary tickets and a fourth of a team signed copy of Noli Cedere. Whilst it is too late to enter for this draw, I will be signing people up for the next one in November, so, bring along a fiver to get yourselves entered and sign up for the rest of the year by pledging £5 a month through your bank. The more people that enter, the larger the first and second prize fund, and more importantly the larger the contribution to club funds for projects within the ground, specifically chosen by the Reds Rollover participants themselves.

The sequel to my book Noli Cedere, Noli Semper Cedere, is now available on Amazon, £13.99 paperback, £1.99 ebook, with all the people who generously backed its publication receiving their rewards at the Port Vale home game on October 30th. All the profits from Noli Semper Cedere are being shared between Parkinson's UK and the Crawley Town Community Foundation, so please give it serious consideration and relive a momentous Covid season.

20th October 2021

Back in 1965-66, before the 55 years of hurt had started, Crawley Town played Sutton United in the second qualifying round of the FA Cup at Gander Green Lane. My memory, if it can be trusted, tells me that we won through a goal of Tsaroulaesque magnificence from our mercurial winger David Heard, only to go out two rounds later to Gravesend and Northfleet, in a controversial game where we had at least three good goals disallowed before going down to a breakaway goal. Biased? Moi? Fast forward 30 years to 1995-1996 and once again we were pitted against Sutton United, this time in the fourth qualifying round. Unfortunately, ex red Jimmy Dack and future red, Mark "the swan catcher" Hynes absolutely tore us apart that day and we went down by four goals to one and our cup adventure was over. I say adventure, but I think we were exempt until that round so went out at the first hurdle. Which brings us up to this weekend's game, and the first time we have met in League competition.

During Walking football on Friday, I played alongside a Sutton United supporter, who lives in Horley, called Trevor. Banter was shared about the upcoming game and, whilst we didn't go as far as to wish each other good luck, we parted amicably swapping as many footballing platitudes as we could.

Which brings us to today (Saturday) and what proved to be a very tight, tense game which hinged on two moments, within eight minutes of each other towards the end of the game. First, the referee finally gave a free kick for a foul on Nick Tsaroulla, and, as it was in their box, up stepped Tom Nichols to score from the spot and win the game. Only he didn't, as his shot was saved, and just eight minutes later, a defensive mix-up resulted in gifting a goal, and the points, to Sutton. I, like John Yems, can't fathom out why the majority of goals we concede appear to be of our own making, but on another day, the penalty goes in and we win one nil playing football. What a shame though, that we lost at home for the first time this season in front of 3000 home fans.

Hard to take, but that's football. What isn't football, is dragging your club into the gutter by aiming racist or just extremely crude comments at the opposition players. Have we not learnt anything over the years? If you were the person who chose to indulge in this unsavoury behaviour, then I hope you now feel ashamed at your actions and feel sorry for tarnishing the name of Crawley Town Football Club.

Hopefully, if you're reading this on Wednesday morning in printed form, Crawley have bounced back from defeat and beaten the Grecians of Exeter City putting us right back into the playoff mix. If that isn't the case, then now is the time for real support. Looking at it philosophically, some people would have been happy with two points from these two games i.e. not losing to closely placed rivals, whereas if we have beaten City then we have three points and are better off points wise.

On top of all that we now know that we face Tranmere Rovers at home in the First-round proper of the FA Cup over the weekend of 5th -8th November. One we, most certainly can win!!

Crawley Town are, in my opinion, a few fit players short of being, not just play-off contenders, but, serious automatic promotion candidates. If I have to give a mark out of 10, it would be a seven because of the lack of concentration at times. Whether up front or at the back, little lapses are costing us vital points and causing us to draw matches we should be winning, or lose games we should at least be drawing. I don't think I have been unimpressed with anyone who has worn the shirt this season but, in what must be the worst run of injuries we have experienced, just as you think one player is the key ingredient, they seem to get injured. Joel Lynch, Ludwig Francilette are cases in point and when you add them to the prolonged absences of Jordan Tunnicliffe, Reece Grego-Cox and Sam Matthews it's nothing short of a miracle that we are just one point off the playoffs. I really am optimistic about where we will finish this season and also think we can progress in the FA Cup against Tranmere. Wins against Exeter and Scunthorpe will propel us up the league and anything positive against Port Vale would really cheer my Stoke City supporting heart. Crawley Town first mind, always!!!

27th October 2021

If the way we lost against Sutton United wasn't bad enough, then Exeter City certainly took the biscuit, cake and trifle. There are differing views about whether Ashley Nadesan dived or was fouled, but there doesn't seem to be any consideration for the third and most likely alternative. That being, in trying to avoid the lunge from the keeper, Ashley lost his balance and accidentally fell over. I am not interested in what behind the goal cameras show, as that was not the view that either the referee or either of his assistants would have had. I don't believe that any of them were able to make a 100% correct judgement and, because we don't have VAR, play should have been waved on. The cynic in me though, believes the goalkeeper might have been a bit put out by the first time Ashley left him in his wake and wasn't about to let it happen again. I may be biased, alright, I am biased, but what happened in the second half just confirmed that the standard of refereeing is at an all-time low in our division. Five minutes of discussion between all three officials resulted in two completely innocent players being booked. Unbelievable.

Which brings us to today, Saturday 23rd October, and another long away trip, this time to Scunthorpe United. They currently sit in 24th place having won only one game, scoring just eight goals in the process whilst letting in twenty-six. However, before we get carried away, they have only lost one more than we have. Having had a bad week Parkinson's wise, I am restricted to listening on Ifollow, but my heart is in Lincolnshire hoping and, yes, expecting a convincing display and victory.

I started to stress out with half hour to go, with not being able to connect to Ifollow, but just when I was about to throw the lap top out of the window a northern voice came through the ether. So, this afternoon I am multi-tasking, listening to the game, typing my thoughts and feelings and also watching England start their T20 adventure against the West Indies. With just three minutes to go until kick off the away audio clicks into gear with the dulcet tones of the one and only, John "Statto" Barnett, and all of a sudden, I feel a bit happier.

Didn't last long, that sense of optimistic happiness, as after a period of Crawley pressure Scunthorpe grew into the game and took the lead on 30 minutes through Ryan Loft, and all of a sudden, we are staring at a third defeat in a row. Good job the cricket is going our way, with the West indies at 37 for 5. Come on Reds, cheer me up even more.

Such is the competitive nature of League 2, that we are now, as it stands, down to 17th just five points above the drop zone. Two goals in the second half from us, and all the other scores staying as they are, and we go up to 13th. Here we go, whilst in the cricket the West Indies are astonishingly at 49 for 9 with eight overs left. If it was in my power, I would trade two of those wickets for a couple of Crawley goals, but unfortunately that's not how it works.

Then, just as JB treads on his mic cable curtailing his commentary, I just manage to switch to the Home commentators in time to hear Scunthorpe grab their second goal which coincides with West Indies losing their final wicket for just 55 runs. John gets back on air but it looks a long way back from here, as Ashford and Rodari come on for Nichols and Bansal-McNulty.

Appiah reduces Scunthorpe's lead and sets up a tight finish with just seventeen minutes left, but even the final throw of the dice by John Yems and Lee Bradbury, bringing Will Ferry on for George Francomb, is not enough to salvage a point, despite having a penalty appeal for handball turned down by the referee.

I, like all Reds fans, will be gutted, but now is the time for real support before we face second in the league Port Vale next Saturday. Don't forget, Noli Semper Cedere, never ever give up!!!!!!

3rd November 2021

Up early Saturday morning, the dual obsessions that are running my life at the moment taking precedent over the more important matters such as family and health. I am full of trepidation as to what the outcome of today's match might bring, but also of anticipation as good and bad runs have to end somewhere, so it might as well be on the hallowed turf of the PPS on this dark and dank October day.

Having attended the Fan's forum on Thursday and listened to John and Erdem speak frankly and honestly about where we are, the only disappointing aspect of the event was the low attendance. Almost to the man, woman and youngsters in attendance the feeling was, in my opinion, that we are well placed as we come into the festive season, but disappointed with the losing run and the seemingly never-ending list of long-term injuries. It was good to see Tunni, Nico and Sam Ashford in attendance, and I certainly got the impression that, even after the last three games, there was still a great sense of unity within the squad. Jordan is itching to get fit for the 3rd round of the FA Cup, and indeed January could see the return of most of our long term injured players, which would be like signing three or four top class players in the window.

I have said it before, but it's worth repeating, support is easy when you're on top of everything and going well, but it is harder and more important when you appear to be up against the world. Whether it be vocal, practical or financial support, it is all welcome at Crawley Town.

Before the game on Saturday, it was my great pleasure to be able to hand out rewards to the backers of my latest book "Noli Semper Cedere" and also to be able to sell some copies along with a piece of artwork produced by my talented eldest son, Matthew. I was also proud to introduce my Stokie cousin, John, to Reds fans, as he played a huge part in getting me through lockdown by sending musical WhatsApp messages, mostly on a Red Devil theme. Needless, to say, being Stokies, John, his son Joseph and daughter in law Emma, were supporting Crawley and not their geographically close rivals, Port Vale. Unfortunately, the game got away from us in the second half after we had taken the lead on the stroke of half time, despite having Joel Lynch sent off as early as the twelfth minute. At first, the offence did not seem that obvious, but if the assistant referee had the same view as the cameras, then it would appear the decision was correct. Crawley played well with ten men in the first half, taking the lead, for the benefit of those who had gone to the bar early, through another well taken goal from Qwesi Appiah. Unfortunately, just as with the Exeter City game, we conceded early in the second half and then, rather flatteringly for Vale, ended up losing by four goals to one.

We didn't play badly, but there is no doubt that we are experiencing the worst run of bad luck in a long while. Not just with dubious decisions, either from officials or players, costing us dearly, but also with the continuing string of injuries, especially to our centre backs. Indeed, George Francomb limped off in the second half, after having switched to cover for the red carded Lynch. I could go on about the officials today, allowing foul throws to be retaken and corners to be taken from outside the quadrant, but at the end of the day we lost to a good side who took full advantage of the gifts offered.

I have said it before, but I will say it again. Now is the time for real support, for without it the players will find it even harder to get us out of our current slump. Next week is FA Cup week and a chance to get one step closer to the big boys. Please take advantage of the reduced ticket prices and get down to the PPS next Saturday. TOWN TEAM TOGETHER

10th November 2021

It may have been the time of fireworks, but unfortunately the closest we came to them on Saturday was after the game when there appeared to be an altercation between some long-standing supporters and John Yems, What was said I don't know, but suffice it to say there was also fans singing "John Yems, red and white army" which shows that one fan's opinion isn't always that of everyone. The game itself was a game that could have gone either way, and, for me, the man of the match was Ludwig Francilette who was good in the air and also showed considerable pace in defense. With a low crowd, for whatever reason, you would not have thought that this was a cup tie with all the financial benefits it could bring. The boycott by some supporters, caused by recent stadium bans, has punished those fans who did attend and the players on the pitch. One also has to ask, were all the people who donated to the flags fund asked for their opinions on the matter before they were removed? The players have done nothing to deserve the boycott, although I do accept, we are in the worst run of form, luck, injuries, call it what you like, for many a year, but, on a positive note, it was good to see players getting back into the team after injury and to see us play three up front, but the goal we conceded was another sloppy one, and for all our attacking play, we seemed to want to make another pass

103

rather than shoot. However, I know where I will be on Tuesday evening, I will be at the PPS supporting my team and asking questions of the club where and when they need to be asked. Sometimes, and I speak from painful experience here, you have to hold up your hands and admit to acts of inappropriate behaviour.

Anyway, onwards and upwards Red Devils, we will get out of this rut, of that I am sure, but we all need to remind ourselves that we are stronger together than divided.

Away from the football, the actual playing of it that is, Noli Semper Cedere has now sold over 100 copies and has actually rekindled the sales of Noli Cedere as well. With 333 of that title now being sold, SANDS and the Crawley Town Community Foundation have benefited to the tune of well over £300 each for which, I am sure, they are truly grateful. The beneficiaries from the sales of the new book are, once again the Foundation, and Parkinson's UK. The work and support that all three charities do and give, in their respective realms of expertise, are invaluable to the people who depend upon them and at this time of year, when remembering sacrifices made by others, it was good to experience the poignant act of remembrance we all shared at the weekend, with both applause and reverential silence. Divided by our football allegiances but united in our gratitude for the ultimate sacrifice made by so many for us.

Back to what, for me, is the most important of the least important things in life, it may take a lot of "ruddy hard" work for us to get back to winning ways, and perhaps in the meantime we all need to read Rudyard Kipling's take on how to accept victory and defeat in the same manner. In between making exceedingly good cakes, he was quite a prolific writer, you know? "If" only I could be as good.

Hopefully, if you read other parts of this fantastic newspaper other than the sports pages, you will have read the first episode of Stagni Ollam et Superbus, which seeks to tell about the lives of the main characters in the history of our club, starting way back in the Victorian era. These episodes will not just be about football, but will hopefully show that we all have a story to tell, whether it be comedy, drama, romance or tragedy and in most cases a mixture of each. I hope you enjoy them and they make you feel Superbus about the "Stagni Ollam" town we live in.

17th November 2021

Well, that's the curtains down on another underwhelming showing in the Freight Rover, Sherpa Van, Leyland DAF, Autoglass, Auto Windscreens, LDV Vans, Johnstone's Paint, Checkatrade, Leasing.com, Papa John's Trophy Shield Cup for another year. The only reason I've included all its former identities is so I can reach my word limit for this week's article.

When I arrived at the People's Pension stadium last night (written at 5am Wednesday 10th November, after another Reds induced sleepless night) I was pleased to see that the rumours of Reece Grego-Cox and Sam Matthews' return from injury were in fact true, albeit as names on the bench, in what, it has to be said, was a strong squad.

Crawley started strongly but were beaten by the speed of the Saint's counter attacking youngsters, not once, twice or even thrice, but four times, to make it fourteen goals conceded in the three group matches. I witnessed all but three of those goals, thanks to my first half absence due to sickness at the Valley, and I am left with a feeling of ....I don't know what. This competition is realistically the best chance for a league 2 side to appear at Wembley, and for some reason we never seem to perform to the best of our abilities in it.

Supporters don't attend, because of the inclusion of Premier League U21 sides, but surely the best way to rail against that is to teach the boys what it's like to play in a man's competition. Something, for whatever reason, we fail to do on most occasions.

I know what you're thinking, where's the optimistic, half glass full Steve Leake? Well, he is still here and to prove it here are my positives from last night; Ludwig Francilette showed he has real pace in getting back to defend when others around him do not, Amrit Bonsal-McNulty showed, for such a small player, that he possesses a lot of skill and a decent shot, Sam Ashford battled away up front tirelessly all night with no reward, but the two most positive occurrences last night were the returns of Reece Grego-Cox, back after twenty (20) months out injured and San Matthews, back from his three-month shoulder injury. Both players showed they were up for the fight and hopefully will feature against Lancing in next week's Sussex Senior Cup game. At the recent fan's forum John Yems stated, that if we entered the Senior Cup, he would want to win it. The question is, will the team he selects feel the same way?

With the Swindon game being postponed this Saturday, because of international call ups in their camp, it gives the team, players and management, a chance to lick their wounds and figure a way out of our current, temporary, predicament. The side, that only five matches ago was knocking on the play-off door, need to show that was not a false dawn by winning at Barrow, preferably in style. This weekend could see the teams below us partly narrow the gap between us and them to just two points from the bottom two, and that has to be the nadir for us this season. I have said it before, and people will probably be fed up with my repeating it, but the most important time to support your team and club is when the chips are down and everything seems to be against you. Now is the time for that support, flags, drum and voices.

TOWN, TEAM, TOGETHER........COME ON YOU RED DEVILS

24th November 2021

"At the recent fan's forum John Yems stated, that if we entered the Senior Cup, he would want to win it. The question is, will the team he selects feel the same way?"

Well, the answer was an emphatic YES. Fielding a strong squad, but missing Tunnicliffe, Nichols, Appiah, Dallison and Craig, Crawley ran out convincing winners against a Lancing team that thankfully made it an honest contest. It took about twenty minutes for Crawley to exert their superiority through a thunderous shot from, skipper for the night, Jake Hessenthaler, but after that the goals came pretty regularly, through Battle (2), Tilley (2) with the only set back coming at four nil, when Lancing capitalised on a game of penalty box bagatelle to snatch their consolation. All our goals came about as the result of slick inter passing and a shoot on sight policy, which hopefully will have been carried over into Saturday's match at Barrow. For once players staked their claims for selection with pleasing and exciting performances but the cream on the cake, with the proverbial cherry on the top, came with the last kick of the game. The Lancing keeper had advanced to about ten yards from the penalty area, when Amrit Bonsal-McNulty saw his chance and hit a shot, with the outside of his foot, which sailed into the net a la Beckham, Rooney etc. from the half way line.

People will say we should have won by that many, against a team so far below us in the pyramid, but, having been there and witnessed it, I have to commend our seaside cousins for their tenacity and their Noli Cedere attitude. This was not a walkover, but rather a hard fought, well-earned six one win which will have left John and Lee with the right sort of selection headaches for the trip to Barrow.

Sunday 3am

Waking up from a vicious recurring flesh-eating nightmare what better way is there to restore some calm other than talking, or indeed writing, about another Crawley Town away win. Sixty-nine vocal Reds fans roared the team to victory against a Barrow side who we have now leap frogged over in the league table. I was unable to keep tabs with the game as I was involved in playing a game of Bowls at Grattons bowling centre, and I didn't have the Wi-Fi password until just about 4.45pm. One nil, Tilley and an anxious few minutes waiting for it to be confirmed as a fulltime result and all I could do was imagine what songs were being sung up in Cumbria. "How s**t must you be, we're winning away" or perhaps the seasonal ditty "Jingle bells, Jingle bells, jingle all the way, oh what fun it is to see Crawley win away". Whatever the ditty, there would have been a happy band of brothers and sisters travelling home by car, coach or train, no doubt eulogising over James Tilley's goal and perhaps asking why the likes of Tsaroulla, Grego-Cox and Matthews weren't in the squad. Well, all I can say is, we must trust the manager and his staff to assess the fitness of the players and make the correct selection decisions, bearing in mind of course that we have a midweek encounter on Tuesday against Newport County to prepare for as well. Two home games in a week must not be squandered, and hopefully, if you are reading this in print, we have already slain the Welsh dragon and are happily preparing for Clough and Co at the weekend.

1st December 2021

Tuesday evening and another night at the People's Pension Stadium saw Reds, unluckily in my opinion, have to settle for a point against the Exiles from Newport. The performance, especially in the second half, deserved so much more with Qwesi Appiah scoring a fantastic opening goal, superbly converting an exquisite delivery from a Jack Powell free kick. It seemed to most people, on the terrace at least, that the improved second half showing was due to the introduction of Will Ferry, but unfortunately, he soon fell foul of the continuing 2021 injury crisis and had to be replaced. Conceding the equaliser in the 84th minute, Crawley almost got what they deserved, first when Qwesi Appiah delicately chipped Day in the Newport goal, only to see his effort rebound off the cross bar, before the returning Reece Grego-Cox hit a stunning goal bound drive which the Welsh keeper did well to keep out. What a popular goal that would have been. Disappointing aspects of the evening? The low attendance, caused perhaps by Champions League football on the tele, Paul Tarran's perpetual four nil home win bet not succeeding and the temperature. Encouraging aspects? The scoreboard is at last installed and should be in operation by December 18th, the terrific atmosphere in the ground, no doubt enhanced by a visiting group of German lads who increased the volume considerably, and yes, of course, the positive approach by Crawley, who outshot Newport despite having less possession. All of a sudden, the optimism is back.

Saturday Morning

The injury crisis continues with Will Ferry likely to not be fit for this afternoon's encounter against Mansfield and yours truly suffering from a badly bruised left thumb after stopping a shot in yesterday's Walking Football. The things you do that need both hands? Who would have thought it! Anyway, it gives me an excuse for concentrating on football and not doing my chores. (Sorry Paula). Apparently, Mansfield are returning to South London today to play us, according to their website. I blame the teachers.

Saturday evening or Sunday morning (depending on the result)

Well, it's Sunday morning, so yes, we lost at home to Nigel "I'll never have to come to Crawley again" Clough's side, Mansfield. In a close encounter of the windy kind, a stunning goal from James Tilley was, along with the scoreboard (albeit not yet fully operational), the highlight of the game as far as Crawley were concerned. Having said that, for the second match running Kwesi hit the bar after the Stags had scored their second, and it would have been no more than we deserved if we had equalised. One comment, that was heard from several long-term fans was why didn't we put someone directly in front of their keeper when we had a corner. I have to say this was a fair point, as all our corners, with the aid of Storm Arwen's north easterly blast seemed to end up in the keeper's hands without too much trouble.

Game gone, points gone, lessons learnt, we must move on as "Town, Team, Together", just as we showed when we all joined in the minutes applause to mark the fourth anniversary of the passing of our former manager, Dermot Drummy. Dermot was, and still is a much loved and respected figure in our club's history. Before leaving home for the match I witnessed, on Football Focus, another tribute to another true gentleman of the game, Gary Speed. The tribute was given by one of our own, Dan Walker, who obviously was clearly distressed about being one of the last people to speak with Gary the day before he died. "I'll call you Monday to arrange a round of golf" or words to that effect was the parting comment after another edition of Football Focus. Gary Speed died the next day.

Having never been close to making the sort of decision that Gary made, it is hard for me to comprehend the thought processes that leads to that final decision. What is clear to me, and this I do speak about with confidence, is that any problem, concern or worry can be overcome with the support of friends and/or family, and if you think you have neither then there are organisations such as Sussex Mental Health 0300 50001010, The Samaritans 116123 or Sane Line 0300 3047000.

8th December 2021

Well, what to write 720 words about when Crawley haven't got a game this weekend?

Firstly, and, to quote Strictly Come Dancing", in no particular order, there are four reasons to be cheerful if you follow football in general, and all things Crawley in particular. England Lionesses beat Latvia by twenty goals to nil, which is still sixteen goals less than Arbroath beat Bon Accord by in the Scottish Cup, on the 12th September 1885, and twenty-five less than Monks United scored against Woodfield Road back in the early 60s. The final score of this match between children from Priors Walk and Friars Rookery being 45 – 17, with yours truly scoring twenty-one goals from the wing. Eat your heart out Ellen White!!! Seriously, the World Cup qualifier victory, although seriously one sided, showed how determined our team were from start to finish, more than it showed how bad Latvia were. You will notice I referred to them as "our team" and that is because of the three lions on their...shirts and not because I didn't know whether to refer to them as girls, women or ladies. Oh, for a striker of Ellen White's calibre in the Crawley Town team at the moment.

The second reason to be cheerful was the coverage, on BBC South East, of our shirts for schools' scheme. The clip showed Bewbush Academy Year 1 being given their shirts by the elusive Reggie the Red accompanied by 16 players, including Nick Tsaroulla, Blondie Nna Noukeu and Ludwig Francilette from the first team squad. Over 1000 shirts were given out all over Crawley, hopefully creating the supporters of the future for our great club. Back in 1956 I was taken down to Town mead by my dad and I was hooked, even though we lost the first three games. My plea to the parents of these fortunate five-year old's is that you spend some quality time with your children on December 18th, and take them to the People's Pension Stadium so they can see the relevance of the shirts they have been given. Nineteen schools were visited on the day, which caused Alex Watts to use the word "knackering" on the BBC. I think we can excuse him though, can't we? Highlight for me though, had to be the assistant head of Bewbush.

Dan Walker is my third reason to be cheerful, as although he now lives in Sheffield, he is a Crawley boy at heart and at the moment is doing his utmost on the dance floor to cheer everyone up with his enthusiasm and even a modicum of grace and technique. His partner, Nadia, seems to have the right attitude to competition and, like Dan, seems to relish proving the Friday night panel wrong. Just like Crawley Town they are always predicted to be "relegated", and just like Crawley, we hope, like to prove people wrong. People of Crawley, Town, Team, Together, vote for Dan and Nadia and get down to the People's Pension Stadium to support the Reds.

Talking about Crawley Town, having no game this week because of the FA Cup, John Yems and Lee Bradbury took the opportunity to have the lads play a behind the closed doors friendly against The Maximum Performance Academy from Ireland. Reds won five nil with goals from Alex Battle (2), Reece Grego-Cox, T.Riallist and Amrit Bansal-McNulty. Not sure about the quality of opposition, but quality time given to Grego-Cox, Matthews, Bansal-Mcnulty and Blondie has surely got to help the cause.

Why don't you get behind the Reds?

Why don't you get behind the Reds?

Why don't you get behind the Reds?

Why don't you get behind the Reds?

Reasons to be cheerful, Take 4

1,2,3,4

Hopefully, by the time you read this in an actual paper, not online, we will have a fifth reason to be cheerful before we make the short trip to the far east, otherwise known as the Orient, to collect our traditional three points.

COYR Steve Leake

15th December 2021

Well, one game down this week and another point gained, but hopefully not at the expense of further injuries to Jake Hessenthaler and Ludwig Francilette. In what was a game rather spoilt by the weather, both sides had opportunities to score, and in the end, I was happy with another point gained on the road. That is, as long as Jake hasn't got a long-term injury and Ludwig can get over what appeared to be a groin strain, which he suffered late in the game, but played on with. Hess was replaced by Will Ferry, (how good would it be to have them both in the same side?), whilst Ludwig once again proved to be a very pleasing player to watch. A centre back with pace, who would have thought it?

Both goals came in the space of five minutes just before half time, and it was really good to see George Francomb driving forward to set up Tom Nichols for a typical Tom Nichols goal to send us in level at the break. I think that will do Tom the world of good and hopefully mark the start of a scoring streak for him. The intrepid bunch of supporters who made it to Walsall were rewarded, not only by a gritty fighting performance by the Red Devils, playing in blue, but were also treated to a free pie and a drink by the club as a show of appreciation for their continued support in the past, now and into the future. I'm sure this was a well appreciated gesture but I'm sure all Crawley fans would swap the pie for three points against the O's on Saturday.

Part 2 Saturday morning

Having purchased tickets yesterday for the trip to the Far East, the Leake and Humphrey families set off for the game rather later than the departure time for Herbert's tours (Beth working for the Foundation Saturday morning) in good form and hoping for our customary three points against the London side. I'm not counting the Quattro Fromagio cup or whatever it's called. The last time I went to Orient we had our customary win at the same time as England were fighting their way back from a disastrous start in the third Ashes test against Australia. England went on to win to make it a fabulous sporting weekend in the Leake household. Unfortunately, the cricketing three lions started the weekend off badly this time, going down by nine wickets after losing their last eight for just 70 odd runs.

Part 3 Sunday Morning

Well, no one had to swap their pie and drink for these three points, did they? In what was, easily in my opinion, our best performance of the season, the mighty Red Devils pressed Orient right from the get go and it soon became apparent that the travelling 383 were going to be in for a treat. Hess was sidelined due to the injury from the Walsall game, but Will Ferry proved a more than adequate replacement, and should have really put the Reds one up before the breakthrough came. Joel Lynch, one of three centre backs alongside Ludo and Tony Craig, hit a diagonal free kick out to Archie Davies, who slid the ball into the path of skipper George Francomb, who drove the ball with accuracy and speed past the helpless Vigoroux in the home goal. One nil Crawley, and it really should have been two before the break but unfortunately Ashley Nadesan couldn't find the target after leaving the Orient defence in his wake.

As expected, the first fifteen minutes of the second half was backs against the wall time and Orient managed to equalise despite not having a shot on target in the entire game. A cross from the right sailed over the Cat, in the Crawley goal, hit the post and unluckily went in off the keeper's back. Were we going to regret our missed chances? No, we were not, as another great passing move saw Ashley "He's one of our own" (Sorry Horley) Nadesan slide the ball into Qwesi Appiah's path and the lead was reestablished. The passion shown by the players and supporters erupted like a mighty volcano and surely must send out a signal that the season is only just getting started as far as we are concerned. Bring on Oldham!!!

22nd December 2021

Well. here we go again! Still on a high after last week's fantastic performance and victory at Orient and looking forward to the game against Oldham Athletic. Sorry, what is that you are telling me? The game is off? What possible reason could there be for calling it off? B***er Covid, b***t Omicron. I had just managed to work out how to get my Covid pass as a shortcut on my phone, and now I will not be able to show the stewards how tech savvy I have become until the 29th December at the earliest.

On the bright side, it does give our injured players a chance to further recuperate and get fit I suppose. I was initially disappointed that we had dropped out of the Sussex Senior Cup because of the priority of keeping players fit for the league, but I know that this decision would not have been made lightly and will hopefully pay dividends in a continued upturn in our league form.

We stand on twenty-five points now from twenty games, the sort of form that would see us probably stay in the Football League for a twelfth season. However, I know, and hopefully you do too, we are capable of so much more. That was shown last Saturday when we limited one of the favourites for promotion to a fluke own goal and scored our two through good passing football culminating in clinical finishes.

I thought I would look back to years gone by to see how we had fared on Saturday December 18th but have only been able to discover two results. In the 2010-11 promotion winning season we did not play that day, because of inclement weather I believe, but we were in the middle of an incredible undefeated streak in the league, which started after our three two home defeat against Newport County in October, and lasted right through until the end of the season. If we were to repeat that sort of form this year, we would finish on just below ninety (90) points. I know!!!! I am a red lens tinted optimist, but funnier and stranger things have happened in the past. You only have to look back at last year. Bolton Wanderers, after twenty games had just one more point than we have now. They finished the season on seventy-nine points and won promotion to League 1.

Further research into results on December 18th has flagged up a 1993 one nil win away at Cambridge City in front of 315 fans, thanks to a goal from Robbie Carroll, and an ignominious six nil loss away to Croydon in the FA Trophy of 1982. Thankfully only 375 paid for that game, with the Red Devils probably numbering less than 100. Younger supporters will probably be thinking, Cambridge City? Croydon? Who are they? Exactly, comes my answer. We really should be thankful for where we have come from and grateful for where we currently are. The away support at Orient last week would have doubled both those attendances.

So, 16th going into the weekend and, because of Omicron from the land of Covidia, it looks like the worst we can drop to is 18th. Salford play Stevenage whilst Rochdale play Newport in the matches that could affect our position. I never thought I would say this, but "Come on Stevenage and Newport"

Saturday Morning

What to do while I wait for my daughter to take me Christmas shopping? I know, I will cheer myself up by watching England put the Aussies into their place in the Ashes. Moving on from that idea, game of patience anyone?

Saturday Evening

Are you a glass half full or empty sort of person? The EFL League 2 results from today can be looked at either positively or negatively. Yes, Salford City and Rochdale have both won dropping us into eighteenth place, just nine points clear of the relegation places, but Stevenage have lost, are six points behind us and we have a game in hand over them. Using extremely red tinted glasses, Harrogate, Orient and Newport all lost and, in the case of the Yorkshire and London sides, are now catchable. The Welsh side however would be three points ahead of us provided, of course, that we win our games in hand.

I can dream, can't I?

Happy Christmas and a healthy New Year.

Steve red4ever Leake

29th December 2021

Jingle bells, jingle bells jingle all the way

Oh, what fun it is to see, Crawley win away

Dashing down the wing

Nadders giving his all

Reds all start to sing

Qwesi heads the ball

Reds fans sing and shout

"Come on you Reds"

What fun it is to sing and shout

A winning song for the Reds

Oh, Jingle bells, jingle bells jingle all the way

Oh, what fun it is to see, Crawley win away

Well, sorry, but the deadline for this article was last Wednesday, so I am writing this whilst looking into my crystal ball and anticipating a memorable Crawley away victory in the "New Town" derby against our friends from Stevenage. I will not give up my day job to become a song writer because I am already retired but I will have missed the game on Sunday because, as people who went to Charlton will know, I do not travel well by road and there are no trains.

This is one trip that I usually make because of the easy train travel and because of the Old Post Office public house which has always been a good place to have a pre-match drink and food. This year I will have followed it on Ifollow, whilst probably playing a game of charades or the like with at least six other non-travelling reds.

Of course, a certain person might have come out with a new edict before the game anyway, which might mean the game is off, or our positive tests might not have turned negative in time, or the good old British weather might have decided to deposit two tons of snow on the Lamex. Take your pick fellow Reds, but if it does go ahead, and we have enough first team players available, I am confident we will extend our unbeaten run to three and start to climb the table. Not sure I am Paul Tarran confident, prepared to bet £2 on a four-nil win, but I can see us coming away with a victory.

John Yems is, after all, undefeated at Broadhall way, having achieved a nil-nil draw there in his first game in charge and a three all draw last season. Let us hope he still is by the time you read this. Looking at the form guides, which I do not usually do, Stevenage have only won one home game in the last five, whilst we have only lost one away game in our last five away from the PPS.

Statistics, in respect to sporting events, mean nothing to me however, as it all depends on what happens on the day and, as the weekend football has shown, referees can still get it wrong, even with the assistance of VAR. I, for one would have sent off Kane and Robertson which might have changed the result in the

Spurs v Liverpool game. I also would have awarded a penalty for Newcastle in their game when Edison took the Magpie player out. That would probably not have affected the result, but for the Premier League to say it was probably not given because the full back came away with the ball is, in my opinion, absolute poppycock. Suppose the keeper had punched the Newcastle player? Would that have not been give because the City full back had the ball? If so, then off the ball tackles and assaults are ok.

One must wonder what actual experience of playing the game some of our officials have.

Anyway, here's hoping we finish 2021 in a good way and start 2022 in an even better one. In the last calendar year, assuming we have beaten Stevenage and Bristol Rovers, we will have played forty-seven games, winning seventeen, drawing ten and losing twenty. That is survival form, but with a determined effort by everyone involved in Crawley Town we can do better than that, can't we?

Town, Team, Together and I hope you have all had a wonderful Christmas.

STOP PRESS

Welsh sporting events to be behind closed doors, watch this space.

5th January 2022

New Year's Day 10am

Just a month ago, I gave up drinking beer because of medical reasons to do with my Parkinson's medication. I have to say I have not really missed it, thanks to the multitude of nonalcoholic ales on the market. However, the same cannot be said for going without football. Yes, there have been a multitude of televised games over Christmas, some of which I have watched, but to be quite honest I would rather be playing Obama Llama or Herd Mentality with the family than listening to how hard it is to play football at the highest level over the Christmas period. Life at our level is somewhat different, firstly our players play eight more league games than the Premier league do, on a tiny fraction of their wages whilst, at even lower levels, semi-professional players also have their day jobs to fit in as well. Going without watching Crawley Town over Christmas has been far harder than giving up beer, especially when the games are scheduled to be played and then are postponed just as you are getting prepared for the event. I would have missed Stevenage because of no trains on Boxing Day, so at least that cloud has a silver lining as now I will be able to attend, but I would have loved to see Crawley beat Joey Barton's Gasmen on the Wednesday evening under the lights at the PPS, not just for the football but also to meet up with friends and family to do what we love doing together. Supporting the Mighty Red Devils, the only Football League team in West Sussex.

In the calendar year 2021 we have played 45 games, winning 15, drawing 10 and losing 20. This would mean 55 points which would just about mean survival, if across one season. However, with 26 games left to play and the sort of form we showed in 2010/11, I am looking forward to a march up the table starting today against Colchester United. Like us, they haven't played since December the 11th but they come in to today's clash on the back of a defeat. Wounded tiger syndrome? I hope not, for a win today for the Red Devils would see us pull away from them in the league and begin the much-desired climb up the league. Little kid syndrome kicking in here, lucky pants on, let's do this!!!!!!!!!!!!!!!!!!!!

New Year's Day 6pm

Writing on a Saturday night can only mean one thing. A Crawley Town victory. Three matches unbeaten now, back to winning ways at home and the first time this season we have won a league game by more than one goal. In the first ten minutes it looked like our delivery and shooting was completely off but, when Tom Nichols crossed for Ashley Nadesan to head home the first in the fifteenth minute, everything started to click and Will Ferry almost provided a second, followed by a training ground free kick routine involving slick inter passing which, if it had been successful, would have produced a most memorable goal. As it was, we had to wait for the "ten minutes before half time exodus to the bar" move before Crawley extended their lead when Tilley and Appiah combined, with the ball eventually falling to Joel Lynch who calmly slotted it home.

The inevitable pressure from the visitors came in the first fifteen minutes of the second half, but Ashley Nadesan found the silver lining to that moderate storm cloud by heading home his second of the match in the 59th minute, from a Qwesi Appiah cross, to put the Red Devils three up. Indeed, when Will Ferry's left wing low cross found Joel Lynch unmarked in front of goal, it should really have been four nil, but somehow, he managed to put the ball over when it looked easier to score. A Jack Powell free kick hit the bar a few minutes later and when Freddie Sears scored for Colchester with eleven minutes to go, the more nervously disposed Reds' fans might have started to get a little nervous, but when the Cat is on form there really is no need to worry.

The winning formation, at last, seems to have been found and hopefully will be just as successful away to the Cobblers and the Cumbrians over the next two weeks. COYR

12th January 2022

Well, that was the week that was!!! On an up since the win against Colchester, life seemed to be getting back on to an even keel, when I saw a tweet which tweaked my senses just a little. I should have known better, but when I saw a message from Erdem, hinting that Joel Lynch had left, I immediately messaged Yemsy asking if it was true. His immediate reply was "?" followed by "No he hasn't" which was later confirmed by my true red daughter, Vicky, messaging me that Joel had just signed an 18-month extension to his contract. Mr. Konyar don't do that to me please!!!

The window is still open though and Blondie and Dallo have departed, Blondie recalled by parent club Stoke City, and Tom Dallison moving to Colchester United. I am pleased that the Club moved swiftly to bring in Taylor Seymour as cover for Glen "the Cat" Morris and hopeful that Tom's departure might mean that Jordan Tunnicliffe is getting nearer to a return to action. I wish both Blondie and Tom all the best for the future except for when we may face them in opposition.

I have not slept well this week, due to a mixture of personal problems and trouble down under. Not medical, I am of course referring to the fourth test in Sydney, which once again appeared to be going the way of our "friends". My mood took a turn for the better however, when, trying to book the audio coverage for the Cobblers game, I discovered it was being shown on Ifollow. Paying the £10 was well worth it, especially as I was joined by five other members of the Red Devils and my family.

The team was announced as missing Quesi Appiah and Will Ferry through injury, with Sam Matthews and Nick Tsaroulla taking their places. Strength in depth and so it proved, as, playing a slightly changed system to last week, we came away with all three points against the then second placed team in the league. Yes, they put us under some pressure. Yes, Glen kept us in it at times. Yes, they had more shots than us. However, at the end of the game we had the ball in the net twice, once unsuccessfully from Sam Matthews and once from the magical boot of Tom Nichols which proved to be the winner. The result was cheered enthusiastically by the 190 odd, and I write that with regard to their numbers not their state of mind, travelling support and the Red Devils who could not travel for whatever reason.

We still only received a minimal amount of attention on Quest, but hey ho it is where you finish in May that counts and I am now feeling positive about the influence we can have on the promotion places, whether directly or indirectly. As you read this article, we are four points off the last playoff place, still with a game or games in hand on those above us. Those games have to be won of course, and that starts against an improving Carlisle, this coming Saturday followed by the New Town Derby next Tuesday and a visit from Tranmere on the 22nd.

Whilst writing I am watching the buildup to the West Ham vs Leeds FA Cup match with mixed emotions. ITV have just shown Nick's and Nads' goals from our victory over the Yorkshire side at this weekend last season. Immense pride yes, but also a feeling of disappointment and a bit of resentment for not being there. At least my granddaughter was able to be there in her capacity as a politically correct ball retriever. Positioned behind the goal where Tsaroulla, Nadesan and Tunnicliffe tore damned united apart, she is seen trying to control her emotions as best as she can. Like grandfather, like sons and daughter, like grandchildren.

I will sleep better this week, because of our improved form, because of the avoidance of the threatened Ashes whitewash and also because I can see an end to the personal problem which has so affected our lives of late. I would like to thank those people who have supported us through this worrying time. You know who you are. NOLI CEDERE, TOWN, TEAM, TOGETHER.

19th January 2022

In a week when Crawley Town supporters have been reflecting on past results it is important to remember that the present is what counts. Don't get me wrong, I was as happy as any Red Devil to watch again the Derby highlights and the entire Leeds game but I have a feeling there are even better times ahead for us. We are still in the top half as we prepare for the long trip to Carlisle, whether it be by car, coach, train or Ifollow with midweek results seeing us drop only one place to 12th. The mood is positive all around the club at the moment, despite injuries to Ludwig Francilette and Will Ferry and there is a real feeling that we now have strength in depth, which has only been reinforced by the loan signing of midfielder Caleb Watts from Southampton.

Someone once said "You start with a point, the very least you should finish with is a point". Well, that's what we did, so why do I feel slightly disappointed. I'm disappointed because according to the stats we probably deserved more. I'm disappointed because I know how the amazing away supporters must be feeling as they start the longest journey home. Most of all I'm disappointed for Ashley Nadesan, because he could have had a brace but missed a penalty on 74 minutes, and I hope he picks himself up for Tuesday night and the New Town Derby. These sorts of things happen, but it's in the past now and must be forgotten about without haste. Another disappointing incident was the shortened introduction of new loanee Caleb Watts who, after being brought on for Sam Matthews in the 63rd minute, was replaced himself, just eighteen minutes later, by Archie Davies because of an injury.

This afternoon (Saturday) I "watched" the game unfold on the BBC Sports Website and, like the 15-year-old that I still think I am, I jumped for joy when Ashley put us ahead in the twenty fifth minute and almost repeated the same leap when I noticed that we had won a penalty with seventeen minutes to go. Just as I started my jump for joy the next input came through "Penalty missed". My wife and daughter-in-law looked at me in a state of bewilderment, but managed to refrain from saying "Never mind, it's only a game". Being a Crawley Town and England fan, what happened in the remaining minutes was just another one of those life lessons I have endured throughout my football watching life, and no doubt will continue to experience until I go to sit with my dad and watch the likes of Stan Matthews, Bobby Moore, Roy Jennings and Ernie Cooksey displaying their heavenly skills for all eternity. Yes, we conceded a goal in the third minute of added on time, but such is the Noli Cedere spirit shown by our team Reece Grego-Cox almost won the game two minutes later.

So, how do we assess where we are at this point of the season? We are just six points off sixth place with two games in hand on Newport, after having beaten the then second placed team in their own back yard and held a team with slightly better recent form than ourselves, once again on their own ground. Looking the other way, we are thirteen points off the relegation places, once again with two games in hand on Scunthorpe. When you read this (in print) we will have also played Stevenage on Tuesday night, who currently sit in 21st place eight points below us, having played two games more. They achieved a three all home draw against Sutton United today (Saturday), so there is no room for complacency in the Crawley camp, but, knowing John Yems and his squad that shouldn't be a problem.

I will be attending this game courtesy of Herbert's tours and Thameslink and am absolutely looking forward to a Red Devils victory, playing in light blue, which will take us up to 10th place with the second-best team in the league, both in recent and season long form, Tranmere Rovers, due to visit us on the 22nd January. I know my friend Paul Tarran will be betting on a repeat of last year's four nil win for another bumper payday.

COYR

26th January 2022

The plan for last week was to win the New Town Derby and battle for at least a draw against Tranmere. Well, the first half of the plan didn't work and the New Town derby was lost despite the heroics of Glen Morris and a wonderful goal from Super Tom, Super Tommy Nichols. Morris made several great saves before Stevenage's winner, which he failed to hold on to, and it was left for Luke Norris to tap in the simplest of goals to send over 200 Crawley supporters home in a disappointed mood. However, we did control the game for the most part in the first half but eventually paid the price for not taking any of the numerous chances that came our way when we were on top. Despite the defeat the feeling was, amongst the Crawley fans, that it was only a hiccup and we would raise our game against second placed Tranmere on Saturday.

It seems that non-travelling Red Devils also felt that way as pre-match indicated a larger than usual attendance for the visit of the Wirral outfit. True, there were some people who were upset about the queues for getting in and the catering outlets, which I will talk to the club about, but generally the mood was good as the teams were announced. Jordan Tunnicliffe was back in the team, alongside Joel Lynch and Tony Craig, and for the most part the team started playing good passing football and more than held their own in a half where neither goalkeeper was really tested. Tranmere perhaps though had played the trump card by winning the toss and forcing us to play towards the Winfield terrace in the first half. I certainly felt uneasy, one of those footballing superstitions about playing towards your own fans for the climax of the game, and, as the game wore on, that uneasy feeling was unfortunately proved to be right, when Jay Spearing aimed his low free kick at the near post, squeezing it in to the goal past a bewildered Crawley defence. Whether it was his goal or an own goal doesn't matter and try as Crawley might they could not find what would have been a deserved equaliser.

Two losses on the trot would normally have me and others worried but putting matters into perspective we are still closer to the playoff positions than the drop zone and we have shown that we are capable of putting a run together to take us up the table. Whether that will happen or not depends on lots of different factors all coming together in our favour. The return of Tunny yesterday certainly was a step in the right direction, but, unfortunately, it coincided with a lack lustre performance, in my opinion, by our midfield. We were fine when taking the play to them and some of our passing moves were outstanding, but when we lost possession, we did appear to lack the ball winning effectiveness of Jake Hessenthaler. During my time watching Crawley Town ball and tackle winning midfielders have always been at the core of our most successful teams and whilst we have an abundance of creative midfielders at the moment, we are sorely missing the drive, strength and dynamism of Hess at the moment.

Do I think we still have a chance of climbing into the play offs? Tentatively, I am going to say yes, but only if we approach each game as a must win challenge. If we do that, then the question will be, will the club be able to handle the anticipated rise in attendance numbers? On yesterday's showing, it has to be said, probably not. As mentioned earlier I will be asking for a meeting with Erdem and Tom to discuss this and other matters and I am sure they will respond in the best interest of the club and our fans. Watch this space.

In closing, Wednesday 26th January marks the 98th birthday of the club's longest serving season ticket holder, Eric Strange. Eric used to be the St John's first aider at Town Meadow and the Broadfield and is at the moment in hospital. I, on behalf of all associated with Crawley Town, would like to wish him a speedy recovery and a very happy birthday

2nd February 2022

Sitting upstairs getting ready to listen to the game for Valley Parade, and I just made the mistake of watching a Bradford fan issuing forth on today's match. His comments of "For a club like Crawley" and "With all due respect", for me are great examples of passive aggressiveness, which I hope will be met with by an "in your face" performance in just under an hour's time. Whilst I'm waiting for the game to kick off, I'll fill you in with some of the discussions I had with Erdem and Tom Allman yesterday. Some fans had asked me to question why there were queues to get in last week, and also the confusion about what was available from the catering outlets. Firstly, about 300 Tranmere supporters had purchased tickets that needed picking up from the portacabin, hence the confusion outside Redz as to who exactly was queueing and secondly Cottesmore School had brought 200 pupils to the game who were all, individually, being scanned through the turnstiles, which meant that access for "normal" fans was limited to just one turnstile in the South east corner of the ground. I suggested yesterday that it was great to see the kids there, but in future when a school is in attendance could they not be counted through a gate and the tickets scanned when the game has started. This was received favourably and will be tried in future. On the catering side, there was a problem with ventilation in the first half which meant chips were not able to be cooked which prompted an announcement over the tannoy (other makes are available) saying there would be no cooked food at all. Fortunately, an engineer was in the ground who was able to fix the ventilation issue and chips were on the menu by half time. The club are well aware of issues with the catering but ask us to bear with them while they sort them out and at the Stevenage

126

game there will be extra outlets provided which should ease the congestion. Right, it's now twenty-five past two, and with a tin of Punk IPA AF in hand it's time to name the team and settle down to another battle of Bradford.

The following is written in real time listening to Gary and Ken.

Morris, Lynch, Craig, Tunnicliffe, Davies, Grego-Cox, Francomb, Payne, Nichols, Nadesan, Tilley

Subs; Seymour, Tsaroulla, Frost, Marshall, Matthews, Powell

And before they could take the field Francomb is replaced by Jack Powell, presumably for an injury sustained in the warm up and Kastrati is promoted to the bench.

Bradford, playing in front of a big crowd, have the majority of the first half, which moves even more into their favour when Joel Lynch is fouled in the 25th minute by a tackle from Jamie Walker, which some think is worthy of a red card. Lynch struggles on for another six minutes before the Bantams take the lead when Cook gets the better of Lynch in the air (down to his injury) and heads home a Vernon cross.

Nick Tsaroulla replaces Joel and there are no more goals before half time, after which Crawley come out in a more positive frame of mind and start to get about the Bantams. Reece Grego-Cox starting his first league game is replaced by ex-Bantam, Mark Marshall with twenty-two minutes left to play and it proves a magical substitution, as Marshall provides the cross for Tom Nichols to score his fifth of the season in the 71st minute and it's one all.

With the game going end to end, I don't know whether to go to the loo or not and with five minutes left the game is held up for a medical emergency amongst the home supporters. After a few minutes the game resumes with a Bantams corner which is defended well, just in time for the 4th official to show 8 minutes of added on time. Not easy this, watching or listening to Crawley.

The tannoy announces a crowd of 14,623 and then Tony Craig scores what must be the winner, surely?

Please God, send the 120 wonderful Red, or should I say Blue, supporters home happy.

Thank you, God, Craig, you beauty!!!!!!!!!!!!!!!!!

Stop press

Congratulations to Sam Ashford who scores on his debut for Ayr United to equalise against Hamilton Academicals. Thanks for being a red.

If you read my last "Thoughts of a lifelong Reds fan" article in the Crawley Observer (or a few pages back in this book) you will know that I wished Eric Strange a Happy 98th Birthday for January 27th and also a speedy recovery from whatever was causing him to be in hospital.

Unfortunately, at thirty-seven minutes past two on Tuesday, I received a text from his granddaughter, Pam, advising me that her much loved Grandad had passed away.

To me, he was someone that was an ever present when Crawley Town were at home. He didn't sport the red and white of the team he followed, but the black and white of the St.John's Ambulance brigade. Here is a tribute to Eric Strang OStJ.

Eric was born in Reading on the 27th January 1924 to Edith and Ernest Strange, clearly an alliterative family, and went to school at Redlands Road and Park Lane when it was built. He then went to Reading Grammar, having missed out on going to Christ Hospital by just one mark.

In 940 he joined the Air Raid Precautions as a messenger boy, and when he was 18, he became a Warden and that is when he first started learning First Aid. In June 1943, when he got his "call up" papers, he joined the Royal Navy, and just one year later at the young age of 20, he became an officer in charge of landing craft taking soldiers onto Sword Beach.

D Day had arrived. Under heavy fire from the German defenders, he tried in vain to use his first aid skills when a young lad was injured in the chest, but sadly there was nothing that could be done to save him.

He later said to his family that he wasn't a hero. The soldiers who died were the heroes. He was just lucky.

Two years earlier he met Doreen Watson at the Young Communists Association when she became a new member. The group quickly disbanded as they spent more organising river trips than talking politics! They married in 1944 and were together for 70 years until she sadly passed away in 2014.

"I came back from Normandy on the Wednesday and said we're getting married on Saturday, and we did!" (Eric's words).

After the war ended, Eric joined St John Ambulance in Reading, Berkshire, where he would attend Reading football matches as part of the first aid team. Luckily, for us in Crawley, the family moved here in 1952, when Eric became a member of what was then the Crawley and Three Bridges Ambulance Division (men only). Once again, he became active at football. Providing first aid cover at Town Meadow with St John. This he continued to do until 1991 when he had to retire, aged 67 as the rules dictated. "Grandad always said you should support your local team!" (Granddaughter Pam).

As well as working as a Photo lithographer at Beric Press during the week, until the early1960's he would volunteer to man the ambulance at weekends, the first vehicle being a Rolls Royce with a silver bell at the front. St John was the ambulance service back then and there was no such position as paramedic in those days.

Eric took over the Crawley Ambulance Cadet Division as Superintendent in 1955, leading to them winning many trophies including the County First Aid Cup and the Drill competition. He introduced camping to the Division, running a series of weekend camps at Handcross before venturing into a series of week-long camps. This was real camping with toilets as holes in the ground, open fire cooking and early morning PT!

129

He progressed into other roles, including County Camp Advisor, Area Staff Officer and latterly Deputy Area Commissioner but his passion was teaching. Not only did he have his Brigade work to carry out, he was also the secretary to the Crawley St John Ambulance Association (the old teaching branch of St John).

He, together with Doreen, taught a ten-week course consisting of two-hour sessions to approximately 60 members of the public leading them to their first aid certificate. Being a man of high standards, no one gained a certificate if they didn't warrant one.

One of his favourite teaching points was the treatment of bleeding: "you P on it" he would say, which of course meant apply pressure. Just a few days before he died, Hannah, one of his granddaughters, asked him how to treat bleeding and his response was, as always, the same. A first aider to the very end.

He also taught First Aid to local factories, pioneering the courses brought about by the First Aid at Work Act in conjunction with Kim Godwin and the late Pam Gould. He could always be seen with his pipe in his mouth resulting in the old headquarters being full of smoke. As stated before, you only passed one of his courses if you were good enough, which resulted in many candidates having to retake the course. Those candidates often remarked that they realised they had not been good enough the first time around.

Eric was also a trainer of Tutors, ensuring all trainers in Sussex were of a high enough standard to teach. Disappointed when he reached the age of retirement, but no doubt proud of the fact that during his 30 years of service he received the Order of St Jogn (OStJ) and remained an active member of the Crawley Fellowship until they stopped meeting because of Covid.

His blood was not red or blue, it was black and white!!

Eric left behind a legacy that will last forever and here is how some of his family of three children, nine grandchildren and 12 great grandchildren remember him.

Steve, his son "One of my early memories of Dad, in Reading, was going to his allotment where when he stuck a fork in the ground, a robin would come and perch on the handle. He was and excellent athlete, well on one occasion anyway! We were playing cricket in Crawley, and this motorcyclist came off his bike, and Dad ran faster than Usain Bolt to give him First Aid! A loving supportive father, who taught us a lot."

Pam, his granddaughter "He was a wonderful human being, the strong silent type with a naughty twinkle in his eye. I well remember Saturday matches at Town Mead, then back home to Deerswood Road for the final scores, sandwiches and cake".

Tanya, his granddaughter "He was always a loving Grandad. I remember him always letting me help with St John Ambulance things from cleaning the dummies, to helping fold the triangular bandages after Nana had lovingly washed and ironed them. When he worked for Beric Press, he would always give us wonderful calendars and when we slept over at Deerswood Road he would sing songs with the one that sticks in my mind being two little dickie birds. He would have two bits of paper on his fingers and he was the best Grandad anyone could ask for"

Hannah, his granddaughter "He was an inspiration, a true hero, and one of a kind!"

Michelle, his granddaughter "He was inspirational, one of a kind, and the best Grandad I could ever have asked for. Nana would have said he was loving but frustrating at times when he would do his jigsaw puzzles when she needed the table! They would never go to bed on a cross word and clearly the chemistry worked as they saw seventy years of marriage together."

9th February 2022

Hoping to have done this on the back of an emphatic win over those nasty people from that other New Town. Looked like it was going to happen too, with impressive displays from Isaac Hutchinson and Remi Oteh on top of a brace of goals from Super

Tom, Super Tommy Nichols. However, it wasn't to be with Tom Nichols blasting his hat trick chance over the bar, after unselfish work by Nadesan to set him up. We are now at a crossroads and it is down to whether we want to turn left or right to enter the car park of mid table, or forge ahead on the main road to the play-off positions. If we can stop kangaroo hopping, then there is absolutely no reason why we can't reach the longed-for destination. One thing is for sure (he says fingers crossed whilst offering up a prayer to St Luigi) it isn't quite time to ask St Jude, the patron saint for lost causes, to intervene. All of us, Town, Team, Together, need to raise our game, starting on Tuesday when we travel to Harrogate. Let's throw caution to the wind and really go for it, players on the pitch, fans in the stand and management on the bench. NOLI SEMPER CEDERE

16th February 2022

The first substitute in the Football League was made in the 1965/66 season when Keith Peacock came on for Charlton Athletic, an outfield player replacing injured goalkeeper Mike Rose, eleven minutes into their away match against Bolton Wanderers. It wasn't until the 1967/68 season that tactical substitutions were allowed, and that was only one per team.

Ever since then supporters have been issuing forth on when to make a substitution, who should go off, who should come on etc.etc. and either heralding the manager as an amazing tactician or berating him for getting it all wrong. The Stevenage game was a case in point when John Yems made some changes which coincided with, but did not cause, us conceding two goals. Roll on three days, he makes almost the same substitutions and we come away with three valuable away points. I remember back in the late eighties or early nineties, when Crawley were chasing a game at Town Meadow, when the then manager John Maggs prepared to send on Steve Norris. For some reason this was not a popular move with a section of the crowd who let the manager and the player know what they thought. Steve, to his credit, ran from the bench straight to the penalty area and bullet headed the equaliser into the net with his first touch. If the tea bars had been serving humble pie, they would have made a fortune.

My point is, John and Lee know all about the players they are able to call on, whereas, just perhaps, we, the fans, don't. There will be times when mistakes are made and that is when we learn for if you have never made a mistake, then you probably have never made anything.

I watched on Tuesday evening as 17 players, numerous coaching staff and 73 absolute heroes of supporters gave their all to gain an incredible three points. The whole of my close must have heard the goals go in as Oteh showed his strength and power, Nichols his touch and finishing ability and Tsaroulla his never say die attitude. Now all we have to do is show the same level of commitment and energy against the Monkey hangers on Saturday.

I suppose it was inevitable that after the Lord Mayor's show of the Harrogate performance we would have to do with what is left after the parade has gone by. Hartlepool , the team with the worst away record in league 2 against Crawley Town with an untypically bad home record meant that something had to give, and in the first five minutes it looked as if the Red Devils would come out on top. Indeed, when Jack Powell hit a thunderous shot from all of 30 yards, only to see it bounce back off the junction of the post and bar, it seemed like only a matter of time before Crawley would score.

However, as the game wore on Hartlepool grew into the game and took the lead on forty minutes when Omar Bogle curled one past Glen Morris and that, unfortunately, is how it stayed for the remaining 61 minutes of the game. Sixty-one minutes because of 11 additional minutes mostly caused by a sickening head injury to James Tilley, which had me remembering a similar injury to Jon Paul Pittman back in our non-league days. I know all Red Devil supporters will want to wish him the best for a speedy recovery. As it stands at the moment, we could probably name a team from our injured players. Whilst the absences of Ludwig Francilette and Joel Lynch are bad enough, at least we are blessed with two other centre backs of comparable quality. The same, I'm afraid, cannot be said for our attack. Ashley Nadesan, Reece Grego-Cox and Aramide Oteh are good attackers but the finishing qualities of super Tommy Nichols and Kwesi Appiah were sorely missed in this game and could cost us more points lost in the future if their injuries are long term.

In seasons past, if we were approaching a run of four home games on the trot, we would be rubbing our hands together in anticipation of picking up twelve points. This season, sadly, that is not the case, but we do have Salford City away first, and we always get something off of them, don't we?

23rd February 2022

Oh my!!! All the chores done this morning; audio match pass paid for on Ifollow, beers in fridge and pictures of Red Devils, Manchester bound, on Facebook, and yes........the game has been postponed due to a waterlogged pitch.

Points to consider

- Was the pitch deemed playable before the supporters travelled?

- If so, has it deteriorated since?

- Will Gary Neville, not that he has to, pay for our supporters' travel costs?

I know this will have happened to loads of teams over the years, and that British weather is notoriously capable of negating the best efforts of grounds men and volunteers to get pitches playable. Those who travelled by GH coaches will probably have their buffet lunch and turn the coach around for the homeward journey, whereas our intrepid train travellers will probably have to spend the afternoon in Manchester before catching their booked train home tonight.

Thank you very much Eunice and Dudley, for he too must take some of the blame, but is it all bad news? Can Crawley Town actually gain from the postponement? Not knowing the team that John and Lee would have selected, it is impossible to say, but my crystal ball is telling me that it gives another week for certain players to regain fitness and to give the management team the sort of headache they long for.

The postponement effectively gives us five home matches in a row, starting with last weeks' loss to Hartlepool, which in most seasons would have us rubbing our hands together in anticipation of a profitable points haul, especially when you consider that two of those teams are within one point of us, two are in the relegation places, leaving only the champions elect to face.

In fact, you will all know that the first game in the run was lost to Hartlepool, with their goal, arguably being scored by a player who should not have been on the pitch following an horrendous tackle on Jack Payne. The result bringing them level with us on points, but with an inferior goal difference.

Next up are Forest Green Rovers, who are currently eleven points clear at the top of the table and with a goal difference of thirty-seven. Last season, we only lost once at home to a top seven side, and that came in our last game against Bolton Wanderers. We actually won four and drew two against the other promotion candidates, giving us a points' gained percentage of 67%. We even beat four of them on their own grounds giving us an away percentage of 43% and an overall of 55% against the so-called better sides. Hence the feeling that we raise our game against those sides above us.

This season, unfortunately, that has not been our experience, certainly in terms of results. Forest Green Rovers are the only team from the top seven we haven't played at home, and, as it stands, we have yet to beat any of them, taking only two points from Newport and Northampton. We have beaten the Cobblers away and still have four of them to play on their own grounds, so perhaps the turn round in our home and away form might pay dividends as far as the top seven are concerned.

If after all that, you are feeling down and desperate, there are people you can talk to, to pick you up, starting right here. I am going to predict that we will play our socks off next week and be the first team to beat Forest Green Rovers away from the New Lawn. We will then go on to win against Oldham, Scunthorpe and Bristol Rovers to take us above fifty points into a position where we can make a serious challenge for our best placing in league two since 2012.

You may say I'm a dreamer, but I'm not the only one. I hope someday you'll see us regain our place in League One.

Post Script

Crawley Town are one of only six teams in the top four divisions not to have given a penalty away this season. The others are; Burnley, Liverpool, Middlesbrough, Accrington Stanley and Northampton Town. Glass half full, we have a great defence, half empty, the opposing forwards are too quick to be tackled.

Discuss, but please be polite and respectful, and remember, TOWN, TEAM, TOGETHER.

2nd March 2022

In a week where partygate seems to been forgotten, for a while, we are reminded of the fragility of peace within our world with the invasion of Ukraine by Vladmir Putin and the Russian military. Nothing to do with Crawley Town or football in general? Well, some Ukrainians have settled in "the finest town in England" and are now part of our community so perhaps we should be reaching out to them at this time of need to show the compassion and strength of our community.

Meanwhile, UEFA have moved the final of the Champions League away from St. Petersburg to Paris, which in my opinion is to be welcomed, whilst Zenit St Petersburg were allowed to play their Europa League game against Real Betis on Thursday, going down three two on aggregate. Spartak Moscow, though, are still in Europe and should play RB Leipzig in March. But hold on, UEFA are now saying that Russian sides will have to play home ties in a neutral country in European competitions whilst the FIFA president, Gianni Infantino, was non-committal when asked if he would return the Order of Friendship medal, given to him by Vladimir Putin in 2019, and if he has any regrets about praising the Russian leader so strongly in recent years, bearing in mind that the initial invasion of Ukraine occurred in 2014. What football needs, what the world needs, is leaders of integrity and the ability to tell right from wrong. They appear to be sadly lacking at this moment in time. Chuck Spartak out now!!!! Like good football teams, countries need a good defense, and one has to wonder if Russia would have invaded if NATO had positioned troops in Ukraine first. I, personally, would boycott Russia or ROC or whatever they want to call themselves, from all sporting and cultural events, including Eurovision, until they withdraw their troops completely from Ukraine. I would also ban Russians from travelling outside their borders. I know, this would affect the ordinary Russian people, but surely that is the only way we can hope to affect change in Russia itself. Hats off to the Poles for refusing to play Russia in the World Cup play off. Up to you now Gianni. Soap box put away, brow wiped down, calm restored. refusing to play Russia in the World Cup play off. Up to you now Gianni. Soap box put away, brow wiped down, calm restored

In other news, Crawley Town and their Red Army face the might of Forest Green Rovers tomorrow, so it's off to bed for me.

As I'm writing this at quarter past six on Saturday evening, that means Crawley Town have beaten Forest Green Rovers, their first defeat for the first time away from the New Lawn this season and Town are top of the table, well, the bottom half anyway!! In the first ten minutes it did not look as if it was going to be our day, but the Cat kept us in it alongside a back three of Lynch, Craig and Tunnicliffe and we started to get into the game with the sort of slick passing football that we all know we are capable of, but which has been sadly missing at home just lately.

Just as we had weathered the storm, Oteh was clearly fouled in the 15th minute but referee Pollard either failed to see it or didn't think it was worthy of a free kick. When play stopped, Oteh was replaced by Ashley Nadesan who, just nine minutes later, ran on to a Nick Tsaroulla pass, and slotted the ball past McGee in the Vegans' goal to put the Red Devils one up. Crawley then won a succession of corners, and, just as I was beginning to think that we weren't going to capitalise from them, Jack Powell hit a perfect kick to the far post which was met by the head of Jordan Tunniclife, who bulleted the ball into the net. Thirty-two minutes gone, two nil to Crawley and Forest Green facing their second defeat in a row.

The feeling at half time was that we would need a third goal, but in the end, despite FGR pulling one back and having a stoppage goal disallowed, the Red Devils held on for a deserved and incredible victory. An all-round good team performance. Now all we have to do is carry it into Tuesday against Oldham.

9th March 2022

Writing this on Wednesday morning, a little bit disappointed with only getting a draw last night, but in reflection happy with four points from the Champions elect and a team, although currently second from bottom, who are sixth in the League Two form table over the last six games. I personally thought Oldham were better than FGR but was disappointed, once again, with the standard of the officiating, especially last night. My message to John though, would be to let the crowd issue forth their judgement rather than him being cautioned for his views.

The pitch and the weather, last night, made for a quick and exciting game and all four goals were of considerable quality. It was especially pleasing to see Ashley Nadesan grab a brace with two quality goals. And with a bit more luck he could have been taking the match ball home with him.

From the kick off it was obvious that we might have a problem with the officiating, as we had a false start with taking the knee, which turned into a farce when the Oldham player, who hadn't read the memo, finally decided to take the knee a split second before the referee blew his whistle and everyone else got up. Seriously though, the referee was, in my opinion, extremely poor throughout, failing to spot the incessant shirt pulling antics of the Oldham centre back pairing. Seeing Nicky Adams playing last night brought back memories of is time with us, but I was glad to see that we handled him well and stopped him from scoring.

The presenter on BBC South East this morning actually gave us a two one win, not once, but in every half hour bulletin during Breakfast. Perhaps the Ref had a pang of conscience.

Well, I'm writing this on a Saturday but we didn't win. For the second game in a row against teams in the relegation places we drew a .... was going to say a blank, but we did get one point, didn't we? Unfortunately, it was against the bottom team in the league and it was a game, that on paper, we should have won. Then again, we don't play on paper, do we?

Whether it was the absence of John Yems on the touch line, coupled with the departure of his second in command, Lee Bradbury, to Eastleigh, or the lack of a real goal scorer up front, that contributed to the less than satisfactory result, I don't know. I do know however that Ashley Nadesan can't be expected to run the channels and then get on the end of his own service. The last two games before today have shown us that he is very capable of scoring goals when given the right service, but it is plain to see that we are missing the likes of Kwesi Appiah and Tom Nichols, who would surely provide both the ammunition and the finishing ability when, finally, fully fit.

Of course, it isn't just up front that we are missing key players, Hessenthaler and Tilley for example, and I do share the concerns of supporters about letting players out on loan just when it seems we might need them, especially when a certain Reece Grego-Cox has just scored a brace against Dover for Barnet. I can also dee the club's point of view about giving players match time and it must be a terrible equation to have to solve.

Two points earned in each game, which of course you can't actually do but you know what I mean, would give you 92 points and promotion. Even if we were to win the last of our thirteen games, we would only be able to accrue a total of 84, which might just get us up, but certainly would put us in the playoff mix. Starting Tuesday (or yesterday if you're reading this on paper), hopefully we will see off Joey Barton's piratical gas men

139

and will be on our way to a fantastic climax to the season. I live in hope until the laws of mathematics prove it impossible.

Ніколи не здавайся Nikoly ne zdavaysya

Noli Cedere

Never Give Up

16th March 2022

"Thanks for tuning in... your match day commentary show will start soon, so stay tuned" repeated ad nauseum and there's only eleven minutes to go. Come on Gary and Ken, put the pie and coffee down and let's be having you.

Seriously though, I'm nervous about today as we rarely get anything out of the Vale. I was confident of beating Bristol Rovers on Tuesday, especially with four players returning to the squad, but we all know what happened that night. An undeserved defeat and even more disappointing was the loss of four more players to injury, in Francomb, Lynch, Tunnicliffe and Nadesan.

Thankfully with a minute to go the Crawley boys start to transmit and I don't have to listen to the "cos keck a bow agen a woe" commentary from the locals who are predicting a four one home win.

Talking about injuries, I watched my son and Steve Herbert play football last night at the Camping World Stadium and the talk, after their seven-three defeat against Horsham Vets (nothing to do with animals), was whether or not training on an artificial surface may be contributing to our recurring injuries.

Eight and a half minutes gone and I'm being told to quieten down as we scramble the ball into the net and go one up. Only 80 odd minutes to go.

Why can't we hold on to a lead? After 25 minutes Port Vale equalise and the apprehension is back. And then Proctor feeds Worrall in the 40th minute and the euphoria of our opening goal has almost fully dissipated. Not finished yet though and Vale have their keeper to thank for maintaining their lead when he makes a good save from Kwesi Appiah in the 43rd minute.

Half time Port Vale 2 Crawley Town 1

Half time cup of tea made, and Paula, down stairs, is watching a film called Dirty John, which has "Woke up this morning feeling fine" playing in the back ground. Is this an omen? I flipping well hope so. Tilley on for Payne. COYR.

I could quite clearly see, on my radio, in the 51st minute that the Vale player, Garrity, was offside when he scored their third, but unfortunately the linesman and the ref weren't watching my radio.

Isaac Hutchinson on for Ludwig and this could either end up as a famous fight back or a disastrous, heavy defeat. We had four center backs and now we are down to one and the score is four one. Not a fight back then. If only I had a bar to escape to, and as I say that we lose Craig as well and Owen Gallagher comes on. Is there anyone out there who can play centre back on Tuesday against Exeter?

At least Proctor hasn't scored. I'm just going to use the oft applied toilet strategy to see if that brings an away goal or two, or even three, with seventeen minutes left.

Well, this is now getting ridiculous as Gallagher goes off with a head injury and is replaced by Marshall. When you read this on Wednesday perhaps a miracle has occurred and the injured players are back, but my advice to Paul Tarran is don't bet on a four nil Crawley win. Only hope that we have pull back clauses for our loan players, as it looks as if we might need them.

Only Exeter City and Swindon Town to come this week, surely anything gained from those games would be a bonus. Almost forgot, Radio Stoke were right.

Having trawled the pits of despair this afternoon, I am reminded that not so very far from here some people are struggling to stay alive facing a relentless onslaught on their freedom from a vastly superior, if only in numbers, force. Perspective helps us to appreciate what really matters in life and my message to Red Devils everywhere is that it is what it is, que sera sera and other grossly overused cliches. I'm off now to watch United play Spurs on Sky. Sons against daughter, son in law and granddaughter whilst in another household in Crawley it will pit husband against wife. However, at the end of the game they will all still have a roof over their heads, won't they?

Noli Cedere

23rd March 2022

If a picture paints a thousand words, it would surely show how Glem Morris was fouled for Exeter City's winning goal last Tuesday. From where I was, sat in my armchair watching on Ifollow, it certainly was a foul, and I wasn't even sure the ball had crossed the line anyway. There are some fans who think the Brotherhood of Officials are exacting some sort of retribution against our outspoken manager, but I would rather think they are just bad at their jobs than be corrupt. However, every time Nadders. Nico or Qwesi "backed" into an Exeter defender it was given as a free kick to the Grecians. Onwards and upwards though, as, if we had taken our chances, it wouldn't have mattered.

The second match of this last week saw us entertain our "dear friends" from Swindon, and for once I was away from my usual terrace spot in Torres corner, being treated to dinner as part of the 50th anniversary celebrations of the other team in my life story. The one and only Town Mead Wanderers.

Organised by John Moon to start off his 71st birthday weekend it brought together a bunch of lads who kicked about on West Green playing fields on a Sunday afternoon. TMW eventually played in the Sussex Sunday League, North Division 5, playing on a Sunday because Saturday was taken up with watching the Red Devils home and away. We featured in our side, the one and only, late great Bruce Winfield, the architect of project promotion back in 2010/11. Players in attendance were Ginger Leake, Dud "My hair ok? Brown, Mick "Snack bar" Fox, Micky "Where's Kelly?" Brown, Sir Bob Morrell, John "Boy" Walton, Martin "I taught Yemsy everything I know about how to react to officials" Hemington, Alan "KGB" Harding and John "only late for a tackle" Moon. Bruce's wife, Silpa, Mary Walton, Lady Morrell, JM's granddaughter Yas and fellow Walking footballer, Steve Preest, dined with us on Saturday before settling down to watch what can only be described as a very entertaining and profitable, for Crawley, game.

After twelve minutes, déjà vu made an appearance, as Crawley's injury woes came to the fore once more, with Jack Powell having to be replaced by loanee, Isaac Hutchinson. Here we go again we thought, but when James Tilley crossed for Qwesi Appiah to head home in the 29th minute, optimism was restored and at half time we all trooped back into the executive suite with cheesy grins on our faces.

It wouldn't be Crawley town without a little hiccup though, would it? In the first half, we had three other good chances to extend the lead, just as Swindon had chances to reduce it and, after five minutes of the second half, that's exactly what they did when Davison broke clear and slotted the equaliser past Glenn Morris. For the next twenty or so minutes only last-ditch tackles and clearances off the line prevented Swindon from taking the lead but, on 72 minutes, Isaac Hutchinson had a shot parried by keeper Wollacott, and, while their defenders dallied, Tom Nichols nipped in to the danger area and headed the Devils back into the lead.

Both sides could have scored after this, and, with the 4th official's board showing 5 minutes of additional time, even I became a little anxious, but on 92 minutes Isaac Hutchson finally got the goal he deserved, when his shot, once again appeared to be parried by the keeper, but this time the ball curved over a back tracking defender and into the net. And that is when the fire alarms in the away end must have gone off as the Swindon supporters, numbering just over 1000 in a 2900 crowd, decided to leave on masse.

Three one the final score, and only one relegation spot left for Crawley to fall into. Nobody has been relegated yet, but Scunthorpe can no longer climb above us. Pessimistic, I hear you say, but I still have dreams of us winning the last nine games and sneaking a play-off place. Keeping the dream alive.

Statistics, don't you just love them? We had 36% possession, 12 shots to their 20, but with 7 each on target. This means, surely that we were more efficient with our shooting, 58% to their 35%, and you could even go further to say that 25% of our shots were goals, whereas Swindon only converted 5% of their attempts.

Bring on Rochdale

30th March 2022

Amidst all the ball of confusion that the world is today I wonder if it's ok to think about, what for some would appear trivial, football in general and Crawley Town in particular. The answer for some would be no, but for me is a resounding yes. Last night, (as of Friday 25th March) I watched Wales, or should I say Gareth Bale, overcome Austria with two wonder strikes. This of course, gives us the possibility of two home nations qualifying for the Qatar World Cup, Provided, of course, that either Scotland or Wales overcome Ukraine first. We are all aware of how charged the clash between Scotland and Ukraine will be, and it will only intensify if the Ukrainians overcome the Tartan army and face the Welsh dragons in the play-off final. As an England supporter I am torn with how I want these games to go but also absolutely delighted with Italy's demise at the hands (or should that be feet?) of North Macedonia. Can they repeat that result against Portugal? One can only hope.

Anyway, back to talk about Crawley Town, and just before I settled down to watch the Wales game, I was delighted to see that Sam Matthews had been recalled from his loan spell at Aldershot. This, I would think, would be to bolster the midfield in the event of Jack Powell being missing through the injury sustained against Swindon. Certainly, I don't think, in my opinion, there is a better deliverer of the ball from the right than Sam, but having said that James Tilley's cross for Qwesi Appiah's goal last Saturday could provoke a debate.

This Saturday I am back in Torres corner with David, Vicky and Beth and even Oliver if he can drag himself away from the X-box, or whatever digital device he is currently using. Back with family and friends, back with people who bet on four nil home wins every game, back with my Red Devils family, back with Town, Team, Together, fully aware that there are people throughout the world who aren't as lucky or as privileged as we are.

Saturday evening 7pm

Well, after the Lord Mayor's show or so they say, but at least we won and kept the dream alive for one more game. The game started brightly enough and when Ashley Nadesan scored at the second attempt, from a prone position in the 19th minute, it looked like Crawley were on their way to a comfortable win. Indeed, if James Tilley had scored, when set up by Jack Payne in the 28th minute, I feel that we would have gone on to win comfortably by three or four. As it was, we had man of the match, Glenn "the cat" Morris, to thank for our slender one nil win. Whatever happens in the next six weeks, eight games, the nature of the victory will not count as much as the fact that we beat them, not once, but twice this season. Even with former Crawley academy player, Dan Cashman, coming on for them in the second half, they couldn't turn any of their chances into a goal, which they would probably have deserved. However, that's football!! We have played far better and lost to dubious decisions, so the three points are gratefully and innocently accepted.

Before we face Salford City away on Tuesday, we are currently twelve points off the four playoff positions and twenty away from the relegation spots. Mathematically we need another four points to prolong our league status, and with Oldham at home to Orient on Tuesday that could be guaranteed if we better their result. I have been told I'm too optimistic generally as regards Crawley Town, so I thought I would say, tongue firmly in cheek, that the appropriately proportioned female opera singer hasn't come on to the stage just yet. However. previous form against Salford is very much in our favour, with three wins and two draws, and us ahead by six goals to two on aggregate.

You never know, she might have made an appearance late last night, with a chance of a reprise when we play Oldham on the last, hopefully not, day of the season.

6th April 2022

With only seven games left to play, and after an unfortunate defeat away to Salford City, is it now time to put away the dreams of a late playoff push for this year? Probably, I hear the majority say, but where we finish this season is important for how we prepare for, and start 2022/2023. In my opinion, we can finish well into the top half of the table or as low as 18th. The players put on the pitch in the last seven games of the season will do their utmost to bring home as many points as possible, but I think we all agree that the task of gaining victories has not been helped by the never-ending list of injuries sustained by our players this season.

Rumours are rife at the moment around the club as regards our owners and I would like to state that whatever the truth of the matter is, I hope it is resolved a soon as possible in order for the coaching and playing staff to prepare properly for a realistic promotion push next season. Whoever owns the club next season, they certainly have a hard act to follow.

14th April 2022

What a week? First, I attend my nephew's wedding and join in the singing of "Woke up this morning" with Matt Jenkins, Adam Fairburn and Vicky Retter and then just six days later, with no real football in between, we learn that the club, that we all love, has been sold. Before I express my thoughts on the new owners, it is only right to express my gratitude, and I'm sure that of all real red devils, for the hard work and financial commitment put into our club over the last six years by Ziya Eren and his representatives, especially Erdem Konyar. More than just a director, he has, I believe, fallen in love with our club, and I, for one, would welcome him on the terraces for future games.

However, there is a saying which goes "The King is dead......Long Live the King", and now is the time to move on and be open to our new owners and their innovative approach to business and how it will affect us. We Are Gonna Make It to League 1 in two years, according to new owners Preston Johnson and Eben Smith, and if that proves to be true, then I guess we will all be very happy. I cannot claim to understand their business, and I know we are divided by a common language, (gonna =going to, jersey = shirt) but I am prepared to give them the opportunity to show they mean nothing but good intentions for the club we love. If you get a chance, have a listen to "The Joe Pomp podcast https://open.spotify.com/episode/3Sill75iRfp81eUwhhlSqj?si=0 g38MBSBR5CKsXCu-dmlgg. They come across as enthusiastic young men who, whilst using terminology I don't understand as yet, had plenty to say about community and history and fan involvement, all of which are close to my heart.

Imus Ad Eam seems to fit with Noli Cedere, don't you think?

And so, as the sun rises on a new era for our much-loved football club, now is the time to put all differences aside and show everyone that we are indeed Town, Team, Together.

Certainly, if the second half of today's game against Barrow is anything to go by, the players are still treating every match as a must win event. To be fair to the Cumbrians they definitely did not look like a team near the relegation places, and in the first half they matched Crawley with both skill and endeavour but, whatever John Yems said to the Devils at half time, it certainly encouraged Crawley to play more of a quick slick passing game after the restart. Shortly into the second half George Francomb had a fierce close range shot blocked by Farman and then Qwesi missed a header which he would normally have netted, but the breakthrough wasn't long in coming. Neat inter-passing on the left saw Will Ferry set the ball up for Appiah to expertly score his eleventh goal of the season. In what was a true end to end game, Barrow could have equalised and Crawley could have extended their lead, but one nil is how it stayed, giving the Red Devils their third home win on the trot. Another positive from the game was the fact that the substitutions did not affect the result adversely, and in the end the win was just about deserved.

What is needed now is for the five teams between us and 7th place to lose every game, and for us to obtain maximum points in our last six. Wishful thinking? Let's see. Still mathematically possible if every result goes our way, but with Newport, our next opponents and currently in the last playoff position, currently on 66 points, a defeat to the Welsh side would mean it's League two for us next season. Funnier things have happened though and I'm absolutely sure that the team will give it their all.

Positivity in our attitude to the team and the new owners is what is needed alongside a feeling of immense gratitude for all the joy that Danni Bulman has brought us in his time at Crawley Town.

Danni Bulman, a true Crawley Town legend.

20th April 2022

Sit down Charlotte, sit down Katherine, it's not time to start singing yet. Not for Crawley Town, or for Newport County. At least, not at quarter past five on Friday evening, and a Good Friday evening at that.

Carol Vorderman and Romesh Ranganathan will tell you it's still mathematically possible for the Red Devils to slip into the play offs, even though it would truly be a miracle of biblical proportions if it were to happen.

With Max Watters in the stands with the Crawley fans, it was Ashley Nadesan and Ludwig Francilette who put the Reds, playing in blue, in to what proved to be an unassailable half time lead, which, despite a second half goal from Waite of Newport, was enough to bring all three points home back across the border. Watching Crawley, over the years, there always has to be a moment of anxiety when we are defending a one goal lead. That moment came when Telford, Newport's leading scorer, attempted an audacious forty-yard lob over Glenn Morris. Fortunately, doing an impression of a cat falling backwards through the air, our Cat saved the day and the Welsh dragon was defeated.

I Rwanda if any of the travelling Reds fans thought about smuggling Max back over the border for next year? Pritti damned good idea if they did. (Steve stops writing, for now, to take his medication and prepare for another glorious Easter miracle)

Easter Monday 2022. What a day!! Another Reds Rollover draw, this time performed by Jack Payne who was wearing a boot to protect an injured ankle, ably assisted by young Elliott Jordan. The luck of the draw, once again, will not have pleased some people, but that is what chance and probability is all about, isn't it? After the draw I was made aware that George, Jake, Jack times two, Kwesi, James, Joel, Florian, Glenn and Tony had all signed two-year contract extensions, the first eight with an extra year option on top. However, there are still some other players I would like to see sign contract extensions, and hopefully that will all happen prior to the end of the season thus giving John and Lewis adequate time to strengthen the squad. On the down side today, George Francomb, Qwesi Appiah and Jack Payne were all on the injured list, meaning we could only name five substitutes, but after having virtually no centre backs a few weeks ago, we ended the game with four on the field as Tony Craig made a welcome return as a substitute.

The game itself was an even affair with both sides having chances to score in both halves. Indeed, Walsall will probably consider themselves slightly unfortunate to lose as they hit the post and crossbar late in the game. The breakthrough though, went in the Red Devils favour, when on loan Isaac Hutchinson rifled the ball through a crowded area in the 69th minute after good work by Tom Nichols and Mark Marshall. The win gave the Devils their fifth win in the past six games, including four successive home wins for the first time in 13 months, which brings me to our current position.

The opera singer, it has to be said, is probably warming up her vocal cords as we speak. Not because Crawley have given up the chase, because they quite obviously have not, but because some of the teams above us are not playing ball by not losing all their games. However, we now face Mansfield and Sutton in a four-day period, and it is up to the lads to treat both games seriously in order to maintain the integrity of the league. We must strive to be fair to the other teams in the mix by putting on good displays and see where it gets us at the end of the season. The same goes for the last game, away at Oldham, who will probably have to beat us to stand a chance of staying in the league. If they are relegated, they will be the first team to have played in the Premier League and then slipped to non-league level. I haven't mentioned the Orient game because out of the fifteen times we have played them, we have only lost on four occasions and drawn once. I might even be tempted to put a fiver on a Paul Tarran four nil special.

27th April 2022

Full of trepidation and concern is not the best way to settle down to listen to a Crawley game. Trepidation because of the injury status of our squad, and concern because of matters I am not going to write about.

Hey ho, here's the team to face Clough's stags, under the guidance of Assistant Manager Lewis Young.

The Cat, Tunny, Ludo, Lynchie, Davies, Francomb, Hess, Ferry, Hutch and Nichols. No Nads, either in the team or on the bench, but the subs number six in total with Aramide Oteh making a welcome return. I only hope that the news around the club doesn't have a negative effect on their commitment to the cause.

At half time there has been no mention of the elephant in the room and, despite James Tilley almost scoring in the 39th minute, Crawley went in just one nil down thanks to two fantastic saves from the Cat, and, unfortunately, a single goal from Mansfield's Murphy on 27 minutes.

In the 69th minute though, it all went wrong. James Tilley, booked in the first half, was yellow carded for a second time and within two minutes Aikens headed home the second goal for Mansfield and that's how it stayed despite the introduction of Oteh and Marshall. Gary Smith, pondered why we looked a little off the pace today. Just maybe it was the after effects of the early morning shenanigans.

The opera singers are bursting into song now, as far as our outside chance of reaching the playoffs is concerned, and the laws of mathematics have finally come down against us. However, we are still a league club and, once the present unpleasantness has been sorted out, we will take part in our 12th season in the EFL come July 30th. The same cannot be said for Oldham Athletic, as Barrow and Stevenage both win, and they were on the verge of going down by two goals to one to Salford when the referee abandoned the game because of a pitch invasion with just eleven minutes to go. I wonder if their supporters would have done it if they had been winning? Luckily, common sense prevailed, and once the stadium was empty, the remaining minutes were played out with no change to the score. Oldham Athletic, the first ex-Premier League club to fall into the non-league abyss. Hopefully their supporters will have calmed down before May 7th when we are to play them, as the last time I was there they smashed the coach windows.

At the top of the table there has been one promotion guaranteed, unsurprisingly for the vegan warriors of Nailsworth, Forest Green Rovers. Out of the other ten teams, between Crawley Town and them at the top of the League, only Exeter City are guaranteed at least a play-off place. On Tuesday we will have nine clubs all willing us on to inflict a defeat on Sutton United, and it is important that we do our utmost to do just that, not only for the integrity of the league but to ensure we finish the season on a high to prepare us for next season. Of course, if you're reading this on paper you will already know the answer to that conundrum.

And now, a little bit about elephants in the room. I do not know what John Yems is accused of saying and I do not know from whence the accusation came. However, I do believe that the whole situation could and should have been handled better. I believe, without seeking to prejudge the issue, that the initial notification of the issue should have come from the Crawley Town media sources and not from those belonging to our new owners. I also believe that people have the right to defend themselves against accusations such as these whilst, at the same time, fully supporting the move to stamp out discriminatory behaviour of any kind in our club, our game, our town and our society in general. I have messaged Preston Johnson with my opinions and questions and, as most of you will have seen he has now tweeted the reasons behind the actions they took and the timing behind them, whilst appreciating that it would have been better to have been communicated through the club media. He stressed the reason behind the statement was because the news was scheduled to be in the Daily Mail that morning and one can only hope the matter will be resolved to everyone's satisfaction as soon as possible.

4th May 2022

To start with, I'm not going to write about what is happening at the club at the moment as regards the accusations against our manager, as to do so would seriously prejudice the issue. I would like to think that most Crawley Town supporters would also do the same until the matter has been investigated thoroughly and the truth is known. Please read the statement made by the CTSA Chair, written after his initial meeting with Preston Johnson, which is now available on the CTFCSA website.

On to what we should all be talking about now, football. On Tuesday I went, courtesy of Herbert's tours, to the Sutton United game by train. Via a couple of pit stops at the Snooty Fox and

The Box Park (East Croydon) we eventually arrived at The Crown pub (Sutton High Street). Being one of the first five Crawley supporters there wearing our colours, I was treated to my first pint by the Landlady (non-alcoholic beer, I'm afraid) and, along with "four nil" Paul Tarran, got talking to a local who claimed to be best friends with ex-Red Peter Fear. Just as we thought we were going to have to talk to him all night, in walked the Legend that is Dannie Bulman, and he thankfully gave us an avenue of escape. After several choruses of Oha oh Super Dannie Bulman, we made our way to the ground in good spirit, but that soon evaporated as Crawley appeared to kick off seven minutes later than Sutton, and by that time we were two goals down. The other downer on the night was the state of the away end, in that what was called a terrace was actually a flat piece of ground and the seating for away supporters was split in two, with a building site in between. After the shock of going two down in the opening seven minutes, Crawley actually had the majority of possession in the first half and should really have gone in level at half time. The second half was more even, but, if we had scored, you would have thought we could have completed the comeback. As it was, Sutton got the killer goal late on and it all got a bit out of hand. Some Crawley supporters annoying other Crawley supporters with their incessant foul-mouthed behaviour, good job I'm partially deaf, and some Sutton supporters throwing full bottles of pop at our standing fans. Some stewards watched while all this was going on, whilst others attempted to deal with it in a calm manner. You will notice the use of the "some" word because it was by no means the majority of either set of supporters causing the hassle.

And then, just when you thought it couldn't get any worse, it did. After having spoken to Preston Johnson, to make myself known, I set about collecting for Parkinson's UK and I have to say the Crawley faithful did not let me down. My bucket didn't rattle much, but that's because it was mostly notes that were donated. Why then am I feeling so down, desolate and angry, I hear you ask? Well, it goes like this. First of all, Crawley started almost as slowly as they did last Tuesday and were lucky to be just a goal down at half time. The goal came in the 7th minute, and if it hadn't been for the heroics of Glenn Morris, coming to our rescue on several occasions, including saving a penalty, we could have been figuratively dead and buried by half time. But hey, that is what he is there for, isn't it? On the down side, we lost two centre backs through injury, in Lynch and Tunnicliffe, so perhaps we did well to keep them at one.

Then, after half time we actually played the sort of football we can play and it looked like it was only going to be a matter of time before we equalised, but a combination of Howard and Brown or Shaw made sure we didn't. Orient defenders? Just as good as. I am of course referring to the referee and his assistant on the West Stand side of the ground, who I have now booked in for eye tests at Specsavers on Monday. You cannot be serious, THE BALL WAS IN!!!! from James Tilley's shot, but no goal was the officials' verdict, and to add insult to injury Orient scored a second four minutes later and another home season was over.

Roll on next weekend and next season.

11th May 2022

A Two Parter this week, starting with the Forum held on Wednesday with Eben Smith and Preston Johnson. Understandably, as far as I'm concerned, the subject we all want sorted as soon as possible was not addressed, except to say that it would not be talked about until investigations had been completed. The responses to the questions asked were generally well received and covered such topics as the East stand, Training on grass (although I trust we are talking turf there), Academies, Sponsorship and even a brief description of Non-Fungible Tokens. There was no mention of Hand driers or Chips!!

Match day 8th May 2022

Oh, I could hide 'neath the sheets

Of my, oh so lovely, bed

The six o'clock alarm would never ring

But it rings, and I rise

Wipe the sleep out of my eyes

It's time to go away for a win

Cheer up, sleepy Steve

Oh, what can it mean that

An old Red supporter,

He still believes......................

So, I stopped monkeying around and actually left my house at six, the alarm being set for five am, and walked through the streets of Crawley to join up with the rest of Herbert's Tours for the long journey north. There will probably be a lot to talk about, with the mutually agreed departure of John Yems announced yesterday.

Indeed, there was, but to be quite honest I was more concerned about where my early morning sausage roll was going to end up. Note to self: Never eat a sausage roll before 7am and then get on a high-speed train ooop north. Thanks to my travelling companions for making sure I was ok, much appreciated.

After getting to the Manchester Printworks, I sat and watched my companions eat and drink with merry abandon, whilst I sipped water and managed to get ten or so chips eaten, without having to buy them a return ticket. We did talk to a few friendly locals, and also over the phone to someone who couldn't be with us on the day, before setting off on the tram to Westwood in Oldham, the nearest stop to Boundary Park. As per usual with one of Steve Herbert's "little" walks, it took us through some historical, if somewhat shabby areas, but, even without the towering floodlight pylons to guide us, we knew we were heading in the right direction, because of the heavy police presence and the noise coming from what was a vociferous, but peaceful, fans' protest against the action of their club's owners.

Once inside the stadium, there were enough police to be socially distanced on three sides of the pitch, to stop pitch incursions by the home fans, whilst the Crawley Town faithful were kept in the upper tier of the away end, with just friendly northern stewards to keep us in check. Just before the game started, there was a minute's applause for Oldham fans who had sadly lost their lives this season. The roll call of names went on for the full minute and is surely indicative of the last two years of struggle we have all had to endure.

The game itself saw both sides attacking at the expense of defending and sadly it was the Red Devils who succumbed first, with Oldham scoring twice in two minutes, just short of the half hour mark. And then, we finally woke up, and, in the space of the five minutes before half time, we were level. The first came from Nadders stealing the ball from their keeper and laying it on a plate for skipper Francomb to roll into the net, whilst the second was pure class from start to finish. Craig found Nichols in our own half, Super Tom fed Nadders wide on the left, who sent in a fantastic driven cross for James Tilley to power home. Half time 2 – 2.

Second half, chance after chance came our way, but again it was Oldham who took the lead when their full back scored from distance in the 60th minute. Lewis' answer was to bring Aramide Oteh for Davies, attacker for defender, and, within five minutes of his appearance, he had scored the equaliser picking up the scraps from a Francilette effort which was just about kept out. The score remained at three all with everyone going away in a relatively good mood and with two burning questions in the back of their minds. Who will be our leader next season? When do the fixtures come out?

18th May 2022

What a couple of days the 8th and 9th of May were!!! After the fun and games of Oldham away, a small lie in was enjoyed on Sunday morning before we started to prepare for the CTSA Festival of Football later in the day. Raffle tickets check, goals check, balls, bibs and cones check, referees check (although we were now down to two which would mean no rest for the wicked) and so, it was at half past four that we set off for the PPS for what proved to be a great evening's entertainment.

There were five teams taking part in the competition. which started with a round robin set of matches which saw Shamballers finish bottom, and thus be eliminated from the competition. Bully's Ballerz , representing the CTSA, and including the legend that is Dannie Bulman, finished second in the group and faced third placed Bare six, in one semi-final, whilst top placed Ukrainian United faced 4th placed Noli Cedere in the other tie. To cut a long story short, Bully's Ballerz and Ukrainian United were both triumphant and moved through to the final, leaving Noli Cedere and Bare Six to fight it out for third place.

It was at this point that the second injury of the night occurred, the first being a bloody nose suffered by Beth Humphrey right at the beginning of the evening, when a rather stupid old man, who had missed his medication, tried to step over (not hurdle) the perimeter fence and fell to the ground because he couldn't get his leg over. It was entirely his own fault for trying to multitask by carrying medals and timing one of the games at the same time. Silly old duffer.

Back to the football, Bare Six won the third-place match beating Noli Cedere, thus proving there would be no familial fixing in this tournament. Noli Cedere including my son, son in law and granddaughter in their team, alongside Crawley legend Ian Payne, Vicky Retter, Dave Carling, Robyn Beattie and Kyle Jordan.

The final between Bully's Ballerz (Dame Carol Bates BEM, Sandra Rees, Tracey Thornton, Ethan Cowdray, Harry Maynard, Joe Comper and Crawley legend of legends, Dannie Bulman} and Ukrainian United (Managed by Owen Pickering and featuring two Ukrainian refugee young women, Anastasiia Kudinova and Viktoriia Hutko.) was a tight affair and ended in penalties, and that's where the mistakes were made. Kicking first, Bully's Ballerz scored and United kept level until it went to sudden death. That's when the United keeper thought he would try and out psyche Dannie Bulman by telling hm which way he was going to dive. Big mistake, as the resultant penalty almost uprooted the goal, it was that well struck. With United needing to score to stay in the final, the penalty taker was forced to retake his penalty, not once but twice, for not having the ball in the right place and that's when the nerves took over and his third effort went wide of the goal, giving Bully's Ballerz victory. All the teams were presented with either wooden spoons or plastic medals and the Les Turnbull Trophy was awarded by his much-loved widow, Audrey. A great night was had by all and £880 was raised for STROKE, Dannie Bulman's Benefit Fund and CTSA causes.

Monday the 9th was an early start for myself, Sam Jordan and Matt Cowdray, as we met at the PPS for an 830am meeting with Preston Johnson and his colleague, Logan. An hours' worth of frank and open discussion was held, the results of which will be made public in due course, but within a couple of weeks at the latest. I, for one, left feeling more confident of our future, whilst still being upset by what has happened over the last few weeks. Suffice it to say though, it would still have happened even if the club had not been sold.

On to the evening, and, with best bib and tucker on, it was time for the Awards evening at the Crown Plaza hotel. Whilst not everyone wanted to put the past behind them, all the players and supporters were in generally good humour and appreciative of all the recipients of awards, who were, as reported in last week's Observer, Joel Lynch Observer POY, Ludwig Francilette Community champion, Tony Craig Away POY, Nick Tsaroulla Young POY and Goal of the season and Glenn Morris who picked up both the Players POY and the Overall POY.

The star of the show though, was, of course, Dannie Bulman, who had time to talk to everyone, whether player, sponsor or supporter. A true legend

25th May 2022

Well, here I am watching the League 1 Play off final but longing for June 23rd when next season's fixtures will be published. What will next season hold for us as we set out under new owners and a new manager? Who is making player related decisions at the moment without a manager in position? When will we know when season tickets and our new strip will be available? I don't know the answers to these questions but I am confident we will know soon, and I, for one, am looking forward to a profitable season in terms of points gained and cup rounds won.

However, before next season comes upon us, I thought we could have a look at how we fared over the last two seasons. I often hear how we play better against the top sides than we do against those towards the foot of the table, and certainly in 2020/21 that proved to be true, with Crawley Town earning 56% of the points available from the top eight, whilst only getting 38% from the bottom eight. This obviously put the "we play better against the top sides" thought into our minds, but if we look at last season, then there is no evidence which supports that theory. In fact, we didn't beat any of the top eight on their own grounds last season and four of them did the double over us. This saw us only gain 29% of the points available. Fortunately, we increased our points tally against the mid table clubs from 38% to 57%, and the bottom eight from 37% to 48%.

Points aren't everything, but they do make prizes, and I can accept that the football against the top sides might have been better to watch. What we must try to do now is ensure that attractive football isn't just good to watch but is also profitable in terms of points gained.

If that's one myth slightly busted, the next we need to address is how much better we appeared to be away from home last season as opposed to the season before. In 2021/22 we actually won just three more points away from home than we did in the previous year and actually lost one more game.

This only goes to show that you can prove anything you like with statistics, it just depends on how you interpret them. However, there is one statistic that we, the fans, can do something about, and that is the attendance. Averaging around 2010 last season, we need to improve upon that figure if we are ever going to realise the ambition of climbing the divisions and staying there. I deplore the practice, used by supporters of most clubs on the

League 2 forums, of ridiculing the quantity of support that teams take away, as I prefer to assess the quality of support rather than the quantity. However, we have to face facts that increased home gates are required if we are to progress how we want. Hopefully, new investment will provide the impetus for the undoubted quality of our support to be matched by its quantity.

1st June 2022

More statistics this week, but this time it's based on the number of miles you would have travelled to watch the Reds last season compared to how many you will have to travel next season. Some of us, of course, are lucky enough to travel to most, if not all, of our games. My hat, if I wore one, would now be coming off as a mark of respect to all Crawley Town fans who support the team when and where they can, regardless of whether that's for one home game, all the games both home and away, or any permutation in between.

Last year we travelled a total of 7562 league miles, there and back, and I know there will be some fans who completed that feat. That would have included me, in my youth, but now I'm only able to claim 850 mileage points for last season, those games being Colchester, Orient, Sutton, Stevenage and Oldham. Two wins, two losses and a draw, anybody would think we were a mid-table side.

For some of us, even a home game is like an away game, with supporters travelling from such far-flung places as Dundee, Cockermouth, Liverpool, Leeds and Cheltenham to see their heroes in action. Next season, the number of miles travelled will reduce by an as yet unknown number, due to the League Two play-off between Mansfield Town and Port Vale taking place as I write this, and the National League Play-Off semifinals taking place over this weekend, the first of which was won by Grimsby by five goals to four against Wrexham. Never mind, Ryan and Rob, that's football!

At the moment, four twenty-five on the 28th of May, it looks as if there will be no trip to Burslem next year as ex Man Utd player James Wilson has just put Vale two up against the Stags and ten minutes later Hawkins of Mansfield collects his second yellow and is off.

So, at half time at the play offs, Crawley Town fans now know they will be travelling between 7368- and 7490-miles next year if they travel to all the away league games. The lower number being if Mansfield stage a remarkable come back and Solihull win the National League play-offs, whilst the higher number represents a Vale win and a Chesterfield triumph next week. In reality it will probably be somewhere between the two options, but I, for one, will be able to reduce my mileage, whilst actually attending one more away game, as the relegation of AFC Wimbledon and Gillingham makes it relatively easy for Reds fans to travel in numbers to these contests.

Eventually, Vale run out three nil winners and the mileage calculator narrows down to between 7392 and 7490, with yet other recalculations due tomorrow, Sunday 29th May, and next weekend. Hopefully, the questions we all want answered, manager? New players? Strip? Ticket prices will also have been answered by then.

Stop Press

Sunday afternoon 2.30 pm Solihull Moors beat Chesterfield by three goals to one and the distance calculator now shows a distance somewhere between 7392 and 7452. Watch this space!!

8th June 2022

Two great nations divided by a common language, and, it seems, by differing senses of humour. Indeed, just as I write that opening sentence, my spellchecker tells me I've spelt humour wrong.

What is he going on about? I can almost hear you saying. Early in the week Wagmi tweeted that because of Steph, whoever he, she or they are, being involved in the finals, whatever sport that relates to, the search for a new manager will be put on hold until the 19th June.

This caused upset among the ranks of Crawley Town supporters, which abated for some when it was recognised as an attempt at humour from our friends across the sea. After a while, and several tweets back and forth, it was announced that there will be an announcement made on Friday 3rd June at 11amPST. Once again this caused concern, "PST???? Does that mean it's a secret? Once again it was WAGMI, and not the club, who posted the tweet, which once again it caused consternation in the Red Devil family.

An apology of sorts was then tweeted back, explaining how to convert PST to BST, which in turn has been received with a certain amount of hostility because of the sarcastic manner in which it was written. Perhaps our new owners have misread the room, whatever that means. Perhaps they thought we could take a joke, although I can't see why, can you? Mark Wright as manager? Who posted that? My rather confused point is that it is early days in our Anglo/American project and that there are lessons to be learnt on behalf of our owners and our support as to how we communicate with each other, when is a joke not a joke, and what is the correct way to spell colour, humour, centre etc. Having said all that, judging from our own Facebook pages, there are indeed some of our own fan base that need to learn the difference between your and you're and their, there and they're. Now that is a joke!!

Back in the day, when I used to walk ten miles to school, through the snow, with no shoes on my feet, a tweet was something a bird did, and that's one of the feathered types, not a 1970s politically incorrect colloquialism. We used to run from Town Mead to Radio Rentals in the Broad Way to see the classified football results after a home match and club news came out in the Argus, Observer, Advertiser or News.

Sometimes, it has to be said, modern technology does us no favours. Anyway, Her Majesty has decreed there must be no news until after her Jubilee weekend (no, I don't believe that) so

I'm going to wait until I see it carved in stone (plastic) on the Red Wall.

And then, just when you thought that we would never get a new manager, Kevin Betsy is announced along with Dan Micciche as his assistant, with Lewis Young remaining on the coaching staff. Judging by what Kevin has written on the club website, I think we could be in for some exciting times ahead, and I for one would like to welcome both Kevin and Dan to our club.

We also now know that Grimsby edged out Solihull Moors in the National League Play off final, which unfortunately means the longer trip next season. Perhaps, the Mariners' Crawley boy, Jordan Maguire-Drew fancied another trip back home next year.

Chapter Two

Close and Pre-season 2022

15th June 2022

Well, we finally have a manager and an assistant, and we also get to keep Lewis Young on the coaching staff. Dean Lightwood, our goalkeeping coach has left, but that shouldn't matter, should it? Didn't we sign a goalkeeping coach a few years back? From what I've seen and heard of Kevin Betsy, it looks like he not only fits the bill as an analytics person, but also as one who wants the team to play an aggressive attacking style with a pragmatic approach to defending. What I would like to see now is the new management team to work on keeping three existing players, in Nadders, Tunny and Sam Matthews and then to sign at least four quality players, one for each area of the team, goal, defence, midfield and attack. I would also like us to pray to whoever it is that can stop our players getting injured so much. Hopefully Kevin will be the sort of person who will insist on training on grass, and that our new owners fulfil their early promise of allowing our team to do so. Whilst at the Extra time hub this morning, I was amazed to see the pitch looking in pristine condition. Ben, our groundsman, with a little help from his team and the provider of the weather, has worked wonders. Roll on 22/23!!

22nd June 2022

What a week for Crawley!! First of all, Zak can only score four runs in total against New Zealand as this Boult of lightning does strike twice. Despite that England go on to beat the World's bet Test side to go two up in a three-match series. Secondly, that great son of Crawley, Gareth Southgate, treats the Nations League as if it's the Papa John's Trophy and sends out a weakened side in a game England have to win. We all know what happened, so I won't go into any further, except to say that we now have to beat Germany at home and Italy away to prevent relegation.

However, I have just finished reading a book by Oliver Burkeman called "4000 weeks", in which he tries, very successfully in my opinion, to explain how to live your finite life to the best of your ability. There are a lot of controversial strategies to show how to spend your average life span, but the one thing that really stood out for me, was there is no point worrying about things you have no control over.

Bringing this round to talking about Crawley Town I see no point in worrying about;

- whether Jordan, Ashley and Sam sign new contracts. I want them to, but if they don't then I trust Kevin and Dan, with the aid of Preston and Eben, will go out and obtain suitable replacements if they think they are needed.
- whether our injury plagued season last year will recur this season, as I trust the owners when they say we will be training on grass this term. There is no actual proof that our injuries were down to training at the Camping World stadium, but you don't have to look far to find numerous medical studies to suggest that this might be the case.
- whether our pitch will be ready to play on come the 30th July as thanks to Ben and the staff of CTC, with a little help from the God provided weather has ensured that it will be. The CTSA held their festival of football on it on the 8th May, the top surface was removed the following week, and it was underwater on the 13th May when I went to the Extra time Hub at the stadium that Friday. In the 35 days since the reseeding ben has had to cut it eight times.
- what other supporters think about the level of our support and the number of season tickets sold thus far. Bradford City were pulling in crowds of over 30000 in 1911, when Crawley FC were probably playing in front of supporters, all wearing red geraniums, who knew the names of the rest of the crowd. Their average attendance last season was approximately 14500, whilst ours was just over 2200. You can look at it any number of ways, they have seven times as many supporters

us, although you do have to take into account that the population of Bradford is five times that of Crawley, or you could point out that support has halved since 1911, whereas ours has risen twenty-fold, if we are looking at this year's figures. Indeed, when we were in League One, you could even have claimed a 30-fold rise. I have said it before, statistics can be useful, can be misleading.

In closing this tongue in cheek review of where we are up to now in terms of our plans for next season, I am pretty sure there will be further announcements this week, re pre-season friendlies, changes to the stadium now the ambulance station has left the site, and possibly even about player signings, old and/or new. Players report back on Monday 20th June, Fixtures are out on Thursday 23rd June, and am I worried? No, but I sure am excited.

Noli Cedere

29th June 2022

The momentum is increasing now as we get closer to the beginning of the season, and this week has seen the signing of 21year old full back, Travis Johnson, from Crewe Alexandra, and the re-signing of local lad Ashley Nadesan, on his return from honeymoon. Congratulations Nadders. In my first attempt at writing this week's article, there is still no news about out of contract players, but hopefully by the deadline there will be more good news to share. And holy moly, if this isn't classed as good news, I don't know what is! Dom Telford, last year's leading goal scorer in EFL L2, has signed for us on the completion of his contract at Newport County. What a collection of forwards in Appiah, Nadesan, Nichols, Oteh and Telford, and that's without knowing about Rodari, Battle and Co.

Friendly fixtures against Eastbourne Borough, East Grinstead, Charlton Athletic U23 and Aldershot, all away from Crawley, with the Charlton game being played at East Grinstead and our first home game against QPR on the 9th July have all been announced. So too, have all our fixtures for the coming season in

League 2, our opponents in the Carabao Cup and the Papa John's Trophy, although, for the Cup and Trophy games, dates are still to be confirmed.

So, let's have a look at what sort of hand we have been dealt with by the EFL Fixture secretary and his computer.

July 30th sees Crawley Town getting their longest trip of the season out of the way on the very first day of the season, with the visit to Carlisle United. This is then followed one week later by the visit of Orient, which will give James Tilley, if picked, the opportunity to test the eyesight of the referee and his assistant once again. Let's hope we don't have any decisions like the "phantom" goal one of last April again, as I firmly do not believe that "these things balance themselves out".

The next game finds the lads on the road again, this time to Harrogate, for which I am looking, down the back of the sofa, in all my trouser pockets, for the funds to get there for the first time. Here's hoping!

In between the Orient and Harrogate games we have been drawn at home to Joey Barton's League 1 Bristol Rovers in the first round of the Carabao Cup, which is sure to be a tough test, but one that will give us a good indication of where we stand.

Before we look at some of the stand out League 2 fixtures, we now know our opponents in the Papa John's Trophy, in which we will face Portsmouth, AFC Wimbledon and Aston Villa's under 21s. I am assuming that Villa will be at home, with one of the other two being at home also. Personally, I would like Pompey at home, with a midweek trip to Plough Lane giving an opportunity for quantity and quality support on the road, to a ground at which we have never been defeated. Am I right?

Back to the League, the fixture secretary pressed rewind, I think, as for the second year running, we have been given away trips for both the opening and closing games of the season, with Crawley Town having to beat Swindon at the County Ground to win the league, or clinch a playoff place. I would settle for either, on the condition we win the playoff final.

August sees our old friends from Kingston visit us on the 20th, which if the season has started well for the Reds, will surely see a crowd in excess of 3000 at least. The remaining fixtures are no doubt printed in full in this week's paper, but Boxing Day provides us with the opportunity to gain our first league victory over Sutton United, whilst the 29th sees the away version of the New Towns derby, against Stevenage.. A quirk of the list shows us playing two clubs' home and away on Tuesday evenings. The two clubs being Stockport County and Colchester United. Whilst the Essex – Sussex trips are almost local; one has to wonder about the logic of a Manchester – Sussex adventure on a week night.

Easter sees us at home on Good Friday against one of those teams, whose supporters think they are in the wrong division, Bradford City, whilst Easter Monday sees us travelling, via the longest cul de sac in Britian, to Barrow.

As I'm writing this on Saturday, please excuse me if Preston, Eben, Kevin and Dan have added even more exciting news for the Red Devils

6th July 2022

Oh, what a week, late June, early July 2022. What a season this could be.

On Monday night, I, along with about six other Crawley Town supporters, took up the opportunity to meet with Hunter Orrell, one of the WAGMI United members, in one of the former headquarters of Crawley FC, The Railway. He honestly admitted that was a coincidence but was keen to pick up on our history. Hunter struck me as an enthusiastic, committed person who only wants the best for OUR club and was open to the many suggestions we had to offer. Add to that, that he only fell foul of the "don't use the word soccer" law once, it proved to be a good evening.

The next evening, proved to be equally as convivial, as the CTSA held its AGM at the Stadium. The only disappointing part of the evening, being the relatively low turnout, in what promises to be an exciting era for our club which promises more fan involvement than ever before. We, the Supporters, finally have a place on the board of the club that we all love and support, and not just a conduit for fan's views as my position of Fan's rep turned out to be. Visit the CTSA website for the minutes of the meeting, and please consider whether you wish to be more than just a spectator, important as they are, in what will be an exciting time ahead.

Just as I was coming to terms with the loss of Jordan "Tunny" Tunnicliffe, we signed his replacement in Dion Conroy and an attacking midfielder in James Balagizi. Dion comes from Swindon Town on atwo year contract and has been their captain for the past two seasons, whilst James comes on a season long loan from Liverpool. James has played for our manager, Kevin, in the England set up.

Then the week took a surreal twist, when I realised Reggie has a virtual, but more mischievous, virtual brother, called Scorch. Appearing on Twitter, he is keen to know what position you all think we should strengthen next. I personally think, it should be in between the sticks, as Glen, great as he is, will need real competition for his place and cover for injury at least. Indeed, at Eastbourne on Saturday, Tommy Triallist, was the only player, I believe, to play the whole 90 minutes. More of that later in the article.

Then we heard that we're off to sunny Spain for a warm weather training camp, to strengthen team bonding and get some serious training in. Of course, being Crawley Town, it couldn't be as simple as that, could it? At first, I thought we had a friendly cancelled because somebody had catarrh, but then I realised it was because it was against a team from Qatar. Apparently, several clubs had turned down the friendly because of the human rights situation in the Middle Eastern country, and whatever the arguments around whether we should be playing a club team from that country, we eventually turned down the game. I am split right down the middle on this issue, because it was against a club team, not a national one, and what will we do if we draw one of the clubs in any of the cup competitions, who are owned by people from countries with dubious civil rights issues?

My son, David, drove me and my grandchildren, Beth and Ollie to Eastbourne on Saturday, to see Crawley play their first friendly against Borough, which proved to be an enjoyable afternoon, where only one player, Tommy Riallist, in goal for Crawley, managed to play the whole the whole ninety minutes. I thought he played well for us throughout, made some good saves, distributed the ball well and came for the crosses. This was especially reassuring as there were rumours circulating that Glen "The Cat" Morris may have lost one of his nine lives. As you can read elsewhere, we won with a Kwesi Appiah goal from a mistake by their keeper. We should have scored more, Super Tommy Nichols hitting the woodwork and Ashley Nadesan missing an opportunity in the first half, with Dom Telford and Travis Johnson looking great acquisitions. Dion Conroy and James Balagizi warmed up with the team, but did not play because of their late arrival. All of the Riallist family, Tommy, Terry, Tony, Tim, Theo and Teddy had good games and the passing and possession was a joy to watch. Bring on QPR!!

13th July 2022

Another week of exciting and curious events as regards the club, but I have to start with some sad news about our former steward. Terry Marshall. Terry worked for twenty years at the Football Club, and always had a smile on his face and was rewarded in 2015, when he received the EFL Individual Club Hero Award for Crawley Town. Some of you will also remember him for suffering a heart attack just before the Swindon FA Cup game in 2010, from which he fully recovered but unfortunately meant him missing out on the Old Trafford trip. Unfortunately, Dave Marshall, his son, informed me this week that his Dad had sadly passed away from cancer. His funeral service will be at the Surrey and Sussex Crematorium on Monday July 18th at 12.45pm followed by a celebration of his life in Redz afterwards. Terry's wish was for no flowers and no black clothing at the funeral, but contributions to St Catherines hospice would be gratefully accepted.

Back to Crawley Town FC 2022/23, this week saw 35 players and staff in Spain, for hot weather training and team bonding at the Pinata Arena, although Ashley Nadesan and Nick Tsaroulla were left behind with slight knocks, to do their hot weather training here in the heat of Cuervos de Madera. Following it on twitter, it was announced that Corey Addai, the goalkeeper from the Eastbourne Borough game, had been signed on a two-year deal. Hopefully, this will give Glenn some honest and serious competition for first choice, and I'm equally as sure that the Cat will be up for the challenge.

Now, the article gets a little surreal and confused, as I am 100% certain that I saw a tweet featuring Jack Payne, not ours, Swindon's, sporting a Red Devils scarf and welcoming him to Crawley. Of course, I can't find the tweet now, so, if anybody else saw it, please come forward to prevent me from being committed. I suspect it was a hoax, unless anyone knows different. Then, following that, Fabrizio Romano, who usually reports on high level transfers between the world's top clubs, tweets that Tinpot Crawley Town had signed Tobi Omole from Spurs on a two-year deal. The tweet still exists, so I didn't imagine it, but happily, in this instance, it was confirmed at Saturday's game against QPR at the Broadfield Stadium, when he was introduced to the crowd, along with the other new signings. Yes, that's right, we have come full circle back to the original name, but, as I believe it's only temporary, perhaps it's not time to change the brown road signs just yet.

The game itself against QPR proved, in the end, to be an entertaining one showing character and skill. One nil down at half time, with the Cat in goal, some of the younger fans on the Winfield terrace showed their frustration at the passing game employed by the Red Devils by booing their own players. While I also found it a little frustrating, surely, we must remember that this is only the end of the second week of getting used to our new style of playing, and I rather suspect that the heat had something to do with the lack of progress in the final third. That aside, booing your own team in the course of a game is surely a no-no. The second half, with Corey Addai replacing Morris in goal, saw QPR score two more goals, the first due to an unfortunate error by the new keeper, and it looked like the boos might start up again. However, in the 60th minute the tide changed, when Addai found Nichols who tried to feed Nadesan, but the ball was half cleared and James Tilley drove it back past defenders and keeper into the net. This was then followed by two more goals, a penalty from Super Tom and a caressed finish by Manny Adebowale, who I hope is given more of a chance to impress this year. Bring on EG, TB and Hearts.

20th July 2022

Another week of happenings, goals and more goals, in and around the Broadfield Stadium and its players and fans.

Following on from Saturday's three against Championship opposition it was off to the OHOB Community Stadium, East Grinstead. The first thing to say is that the pitch looked superb, which is no surprise as Ben, our grounds man, looks after it as well as he does the Broadfield playing surface. The team in the first half consisted of five triallists, Corey Addai, Ronan Silva, Manny Adebowale, Harry Ransom, Owen Gallacher and skipper for the night, Mark Marshall.

Playing a passing, high press game, Crawley Town were four up at half time. Two behind the Lionesses playing Norway down at the Amex, to which a fair few Crawley supporters had travelled. In the second half Rafiq Khaleel, Mustafa Hussein, Florian Kastrati, Szymon Kowalczyk and two more triallists were introduced, and in the end, only Adebowale and Ransom completed the whole 90 minutes. The speed and intensity of the Crawley team never abated and the final score was nine nil, with all the goals being scored by the triallists, including four from one of them, thought to be Jayden Davis, ex Millwall U23 player. A great balmy evening, made better by the lionesses' demolition

172

of Norway by eight goals to nil. Jonas Gar Store, Jonas Gar Store, your girls took a hell of a beating.

On to Three Bridges, and with a starting lineup featuring just two triallists, once again the passing game was employed to great effect. Goals from Tilley, Appiah and Nadesan saw the greys (new kit please?) go in three up at half time with further goals being added after the break, by Nadesan and Oteh. All our five forwards had opened their accounts except for Dom Telford. Never fear though, as Dom Telford superbly made Oteh's chance and will, no doubt, find the back of the net before too long.

Most of you will know that I cannot make long journeys anymore, so Northampton will probably be the furthest away game I will be going to this season, but I was able to be in Edinburgh on Saturday, at least in spirit, thanks to Hearts TV. Last season, Hearts finished in third place in the Scottish Premier League, but 28 and 32 points behind the runners up, Glasgow Rangers, and the champions Glasgow Celtic, respectively. The reward for them, being a place in the Europa League.

Well, another example that we won't give up on anything this season, long may it continue. The character I mean, not the going behind. Two nil down at half time to two Kingsley goals, Crawley came out in a resolute manner in the second half and, within seven minutes, were level through two Dom Telford goals, getting off his mark in superb style. Indeed, we could have been ahead in the 54th minute when Tom Nichols was denied by a last-ditch tackle. The game then lost a bit of fluidity as both sides brought on numerous subs in an attempt to win the game. The match finished two all and the first Telford goal was set up by Rob Hunt ex Swindon right back. Has he signed? Scottish Premier League? Scotland's number one in goal? Roll on Tuesday, and every other match day in what promises to be an exciting season.

27th July 2022

Third time I've written this, but that's football, ever changing. Having been at Aldershot, I hope lessons have been learnt about when to play short intricate passes and when not to. But, as my dad used to say, "if you've never made a mistake, you've never tried to make anything". A blessing in disguise, this result might just help to keep our feet on the ground as far as expectations are concerned. I am incredibly positive about this season, but with a few questions such as; where is Nick Tsaroulla, why are we not training on grass as promised, and where is our kit? They do need answering, and I'm sure they will be. Tsaroulla was going to be my tip for player of the season, but in his absence, I will go for Super Tommy Nichols. I am sure we will improve on last season's finish of twelfth and predict we will also get past the first hurdle in all the cup competitions. Who will play in goal will be the big question for Kevin to come up with an answer to, and I'm sure the supporters will be split as to whether or not he gets that decision right. Remember, Noli Cedere and Town, Team, Together, Players, Management and Supporters.

Chapter Three

2022/2023

Here are the results for the 2022/2023, but this time there is the opportunity to dig deep into your memories to fill in the missing information.

30/7/2022	Carlisle United 1–0	Crawley Town	
6/8/2022	Crawley Town 0–1	Leyton Orient	
13/8/2022	Harrogate Town	0–0	Crawley Town
16/8/ 2022	Crawley Town 2–3	Northampton Town	
20 /8/2022	Crawley Town 0–2	AFC Wimbledon	
27/8/2022	Rochdale	1–1	Crawley Town
3/9/2022	Salford City	2–2	Crawley Town
10/9 2022	Crawley Town PP	Gillingham	
13 /9/2022	Crawley Town 3–2	Stockport County	

17/9/2022	Crewe Alex'dra	1–0	Crawley Town
24 /9/2022	D'caster Rovers	4–1	Crawley Town
1 /10/ 2022	Crawley Town	1–2	Stevenage
8 /10/ 2022	Grimsby Town	3–0	Crawley Town
15 /10/ 2022	Crawley Town	2–1	Newport County
22 /10/ 2022	Crawley Town	3–2	Mansfield Town
25 /10/ 2022	Colchester Utd	2–2	Crawley Town
29 /10/2022	Bradford City	1–1	Crawley Town
12 /11/ 2022	Crawley Town	1–0	Barrow
19 /11/ 2022	Walsall	2–1	Crawley Town
22 /11/ 2022	Crawley Town	0–0	Gillingham
3 /12/ 2022	Crawley Town	2–0	Swindon Town

9 /12/ 2022	Crawley Town	0–2	Hartlepool United
17 /12/ 2022	Tranmere	PP	Crawley Town
26 /12/ 2022	Crawley Town	1–2	Sutton United
30 /12/ 2022	Stevenage	3–1	Crawley Town
2 /1 / 2023	Newport Cty	2–2	Crawley Town
14 /1/ 2023	Crawley Town	PP	Doncaster Rovers
21/1/ 2023	Sutton United	PP	Crawley Town
24/1/ 2023	Crawley Town	PP	Grimsby Town
28/ 1/ 2023	Crawley Town	3–2	Salford City
4 /2/2023	Gillingham	1–0	Crawley Town
11/ 2/ 2023	Crawley Town	2–2	Crewe Alexandra
14/ 2/ 2023	Stockport Cty	2–1	Crawley Town

18/ 2/ 2023	Leyton Orient	1–0	Crawley Town
25/ 2/ 2023	Crawley Town	2–5	Carlisle United
28/2/2023	Tranmere	1–0	Crawley Town
4/ 3/ 2023	Northampton	1–0	Crawley Town
7 / 3/ 2023	Sutton United	3–0	Crawley Town
11/ 3/ 2023	Crawley Town	3–1	Harrogate Town
18/ 3/ 2023	AFC KIngston	0–1	Crawley Town
21/ 3/ 2023	Crawley Town	1–1	Doncaster Rovers
25/ 3/ 2023	Crawley Town	2–0	Rochdale
28/ 3/ 2023	Crawley Town	1–1	Grimsby Town
1/ 4/ 2023	Mansfield	4–1	Crawley Town
7/ 4/2023	Crawley Town	0–0	Bradford City

10 / 4/ 2023	Barrow	4–0	Crawley Town
15/ 4/ 2023	Crawley Town	2–1	Tranmere Rovers
18 /4/ 2023	Crawley Town	0–0	Colchester United
22/ 4/ 2023	Hartlepool Utd	0–2	Crawley Town
29 /4/ 2023	Crawley Town	0–0	Walsall
8/5 / 2023	Swindon Town	2 - 1	Crawley Town

3rd August 2022

Well. first of all, let me say I was not one of the incredible 166 fans who travelled to Carlisle, whether it be from Liverpool, Cockermouth, Yorkshire or Crawley. I listened to the game courtesy of Ifollow, and got a taste, from Phil and Ken, that it wasn't the best of performances. However, you can't really blame playing it out from the back as the reason for our defeat, can you? The goal, now witnessed by me on the Sky highlights appeared to be the result of our defenders trying to boot the ball clear, a la John Smith's "Ave It" style, and not connecting properly. My heart goes out to all that travelled, especially with the chaos on the trains or having to spend nearly all day on the coach, for 90 minutes of football and no shots on target. I'm sure there are those, who on waking up this morning, will have a slightly different view of the game than they had yesterday for whatever reason, be that a good night's kip or a few hours without alcohol. Don't get me wrong, I was disappointed with the result but am cheered by the fact that we did, as Kevin pointed out, have the majority of possession. However, we now need to convert that into chances, off target into on target, on target into goals. I guess what I'm trying to say is, we have started as we did last year with an away defeat, which is one of the three results that were up for grabs yesterday, and we now have a week to sort out any areas of weakness before we entertain Orient next Saturday. Unfortunately, there will be no goal line technology available for that game.

With forwards such as Appiah, Nadesan, Telford and Nichols, I am sure it won't be long before we start banging in the goals, and I'm more concerned as to whether we need to find another keeper depending on the seriousness of Balcombe's injury. Apparently, there is a vastly experienced keeper at Gillingham that might fit the bill if needed.

There are rumours that there could be more movement, both in and out, before the window closes, so I am not going to use my league ladders handout (available in the Tiger circa 1966) until the end of September at the earliest. To use a Dad's Army analogy, I suppose how you view things at the moment depends on whether you're a Private Fraser, Corporal Jones or a Pike type character. Are you "We're all doooooomed, I tell ya, we're all doooooomed" or a "Don't panic, Capt Mainwaring, Don't Panic". You might be like my good friend Paul "stupid boy, Pike" Tarran who regularly puts money on us winning four nil. However you are feeling, on the day football prepares to start the journey home, just remember everything will be alright in the end, and if it's not alright, it's not the end. (You can insert any suitable football related platitude you like here}

Stop press: Football is coming home, my good friend Carol Bates BEM was lucky enough to be at Wembley to witness it. Well done to all the Lionesses who beat the Germans in a memorable game that has done such a lot, not just for women's football, but for the whole nation.

10th August 2022

The lesson today is taken from the **Gospel of Matthew**, "The last shall be first and the first last." Leyton Orient featured in our last home game of last season, and were our guests today for our first home game of this season. We all know that we should have drawn last season's game courtesy of James Tilley's "goal", but ended up conceding a second in injury time and losing two nil. Unfortunately, today's bible reading didn't change the result from last year into a home victory and, in a cruel ironic twist, it was Tilley's missed chance in the first half that gave Orient the opportunity to win the game in the second. I firmly believe, that if that first half chance had gone in, we would have got something from the game. I also believe that all of us, the fans that is, need to realise that patience is a virtue which we don't seem to have at the moment. Look at the highlights of the game and you will see that Tilley's chance, which normally he would have finished with ease, came at the end of a flowing seven man move from one end of the pitch to the other. Listen to Kevin Betsy's analysis of the game and, I hope, you will hear the frustration in his voice at the way we didn't take the momentum into the final third as much as we should, but also the acceptance that some of our own supporters turned on the team when perhaps support was needed the most. Town, that's you and me and the 3000-home support from yesterday, Team, the players and coaches and club staff, Together, through the good times and the "bad" will, I am absolutely sure, see us rise up the table soon.

Contrary to popular belief, I try and be impartial when writing about how we have performed and, to try and prove the point, I will admit that I was as disappointed with the result as any home fan was on Saturday, but to start booing and even chanting against my own team, is, I am proud to say, not in my nature. I am sure this is also true of the vast majority of our support, but, if it isn't true of you, perhaps you should remember that we are just two games in to a 46-game season. Starting my sixty seventh year of watching the Red Devils, I am lucky to have witnessed all five of our promotion seasons, none of which, I believe, have started with a first game victory. Indeed, our relegation season,

2014/15 saw us top of the table on six points after the first two games but ultimately ended with us going down on the final day.

Where to now? I can almost hear you say. Well, I hope we have beaten Bristol Rovers on Tuesday in the Carabao cup, but whatever the result I will be following the team on Ifollow against Harrogate and will be back at the Broadfield on the 16th August to see us play the Cobblers. Will you?

17th August 2022

What a difference 3 days make, 77 little hours. Following on from the disappointment of last Saturday, a much-improved performance saw us gain a well-earned victory over Joey Barton's Gas. Actually, from where I was standing, behind my red tinted glasses, I think we should have won by more. Super Tom's chance in the first half, and Oteh's effort which just clipped the outside of the far post after the interval, would have given it a much fairer impression of how well we played. Tom showed his class with his finish, and although the front on view of Jack Powell did seem to show a handball, that wasn't the view any of the officials had. What are they supposed to do Joey? Take your word for it?

The biggest positives for me, were how well the "old" boys played our new method of playing, but with common sense when needed, and how well Corey Addai played in goal, commanding his box, catching everything and also making a couple of good saves to keep the clean sheet. The statistics were pretty even, but pleasingly our shots score, both on and off target, showed an improvement over the first two games. The one negative was the size of the crowd, and as a result I wonder if the club might consider using the same pricing strategy that they employed for the 2019 League cup run when we pulled in nearly 15000 fans in the three home games that we played.

Hats off to those who travelled to the Tea room capital of the world on Saturday. Whether you travelled by coach, car or managed to find a circuitous train route which avoided the train driver's dispute, you should be saluted. I, as with Carlisle, was once again listening to the dulcet tones of Gary Smith and "Travel" Ken Blackmore and was glad to see that only two changes had been made to the team that beat Bristol Rovers. George Francomb and Dion Conroy missing out because of injuries. As I have said before, listening to the game puts you through as much stress as if you are actually there and by the end of the ninety minutes, I was very willing to accept the point gained away from home. This was even better received because of results from elsewhere moving us out of the relegation places. Before you tell me to practice what I preach, exercising patience before judging our prospects, I have to admit that I, just like the rest of you, am anxious to see the first league goal go in, the first victory won and us rise up the table. Personally, I don't think it will be too long before all of that happens and I am gladdened to see that our defence seems to be more resolute as each game goes on, only two goals conceded in four games. However, the injury situation does concern me as we are definitely under pressure at the back with at least three centre backs on the injury list, including the latest casualty, Ludwig Francilette.

Here's hoping that, by the time you read this in print, some of our injured are fit again and we have beaten the cobblers.

24th August 2022

Well, I got one half of my wish in last week's article granted against Northampton last week, in that James Ballagizi scored not only our first goal of the league season, but our second as well. Indeed, If Nadders had added to his two assists the goals he would normally have slotted away, we would have won comfortably. Disappointed, but not downhearted as I am sure the upturn in fortune and results will come shortly. Now please excuse me as I prepare for the much-anticipated AFC Wimbledon match and the purchase of my new first team shirt.

Well, what can you say about that, except that the only positive I personally took from this afternoon (Saturday) was the social interaction with friends and family and the purchase of the new home shirt. I suspected we might be in for a tough afternoon after I noticed two proof reading errors in the programme, one including a reference to Northampton and the other saying that the last time we had played AFC was in the FA Cup and, although the match report was correct, the headline had us losing 2-1. The afternoon just got worse from there on in, with the Red Devils gifting AFC with two goals after a promising first five minutes. The performance, in front of a 3800 crowd, was abject to say the least and at half time this prompted Kevin Betsy into making three changes Tilley, Bremang and Ransom on for Powell, Adebowale and Jenks, but whatever that was supposed to achieve, was dealt a devasting blow in the 55th minute when Tony Craig, for me town's best player on the day, was "awarded" a second yellow card. Some might like to think that the ten men did extremely well to stop AFC from getting more goals, but for me I would rather have lost by more trying to get back into the game. There were boos at the end of the game, which I will never join in with, but I can understand why people, especially new supporters lured by the promise of fast attacking football, would react in such a manner.

Two things to ponder over the next week;

1. The crowd was again a good size, but that was in part due to the 1200 away supporters present with the home support down by approximately 500 since the Orient game.

2. Next week, after just five games we are involved in a real bottom of the table clash against Rochdale, who are the only team keeping us off bottom place.

I, for one, would like to see us get out of the perilous position we are in by playing attractive passing football with Betsy in charge, but I fear that there will be calls for a change in management before very much longer if this poor run continues. Not going to judge anyone by the result against Fulham, as, in our current position a league victory, up north the following Saturday, would be of more value.

I'll end with a platitude, apologies for that.

Everything will be ok in the end, and if it's not ok, it's not the end.

31st August 2022

Looking on the positive side of things over the last week against the negatives as per a balance sheet perhaps we could make a judgement as to whether we need to go cap in hand to someone who can help us out of our doldrums or stick with our present approach and wait for the inevitable upturn. I say inevitable because I think we are not far off it now.

Positive v Negative

An incredible performance against Premier League Fulham with difficulty in naming a man of the match. Two cracking goals scored, one each for Super Tommy Nichols and the irrepressible James Balagizi coupled with a clean sheet from Corey Addai and, as he points out, the rest of the team filled me with an immense amount of pride. However, the pitch invasion, whilst entirely understandable, did cause me some frustration in that it will inevitably lead to a sanction from the EFL, which hopefully will be only financial. There will come a time, I am sure, when points will be deducted, grounds closed or cup disqualifications imposed. I can hear the computers being switched on and the tweets being sent out to point out that Tuesday's incident was encouraged by our owners, largely good spirited in nature but I can also sense the frustrations in our grounds man as he had to witness parents taking their smaller children onto the pitch for them to practice knee slides on the pitch. The last negative being that it took away, from those in the stands, the ability to applaud their heroes because they simply could not see them.

Follow that with the reward of Burnley away on November 7th/8th I'm not sure whether that is a plus or a minus. A plus for me, as I've never been there, a negative as it probably won't bring in any TV revenue. Anyway, that's a long way off, 9 ½ weeks, (good title for a film), 5 home league games, 6 away, 3

PapaJohnsLDVFreightroverJohnstonesPaint cup matches and even one FA cup Match to consider before then, to be precise.

So, after the Lord Mayor's show a match, which was somewhat unfairly, I feel, labelled as a relegation six pointer and one that might call for a change in our management from some of our fickle fans. It ended in a one all draw with Jack Powell scoring a great goal in first half injury time, ably assisted by James Balagizi but with 'Dale earning their first point of the season with a second half equaliser. All I have seen of the game is the very short highlight's clip, and I have to say that I think Nick Tsaroulla was very harshly dealt with over his second yellow card, as it appeared that the Rochdale lad stumbled a good foot after Nick's "tackle". Positives? A point away from home, two matches undefeated on the trot way from home, and at least another 80 minutes played by Nick Tsaroulla (who can now have a one game rest, which I don't think will be the game against Pompey unfortunately). Negatives, for me, the reaction of some of our fans, who almost certainly were patting Betsy on the back on Tuesday.

7th September 2022

A win, albeit after penalties, followed by a good, yes, a good point at Salford on Saturday, points I think, to us approaching the corner. Now all we have to do, is turn it.

Of course, I am only going on watching the home game and following on Ifollow the away game. However, if we had been level with Salford on points and held them to a draw at their place, I would have said that was a good point too. Surely that makes Saturday's result even better. Yes, we need a win but let's look at what we have achieved so far in all matches.

L, W, L, D, L, L, W, D, W/D, D

I know what people will be saying "There goes Steve, putting on his red tinted specs again", but I have to say I would rather wear those than look at games through the bottom of beer bottles (only joking). Encouragement to achieve is the best form of support you can give people, if you want them to be motivated to improve. Our squad is full of impressionable young players, who no doubt are more social media aware than a geriatric supporter like me. So next time you want to bemoan their ability, why not do it in a positive manner, rather than a negative one. Speaking as a retired teacher, I know that approach works, and I'm pretty sure it would also work in the football environment.

Going back to the Salford game, a cracking goal by Super Tommy Nichols and a scrambled effort by Ludwig earned us a valuable point against a team that hadn't conceded at home and, were in fact, looking for their fourth straight home win. So, how then can our result against them be seen as two points lost, rather than one gained. Forget the "start with a point, finish with at least a point" philosophy. Both teams start with 0 points. meaning you can only gain points in any game by drawing or winning. I do accept that it can feel like you've dropped points, but when you've come from behind, not once, but twice, how can that be anything other than gaining a point.

Looking back even further to the Portsmouth game, I watched from the West Stand for once and was pleased with the commitment and attitude shown by all our players with James Tilley, for me, putting in a match winning display, despite missing his penalty in the shoot-out. James won both of the penalties in normal time, neither of which appeared to be controversial as attested to by the Pompey media. I also think that David Bremang, David Robson and Rafiq Khaleel deserve special mention, Bremang for taking and scoring two penalties, Robson for saving Freeman's attempt and cool as ice Rafiq for slotting home the winning kick.

Will we actually qualify for the knockout stages of the Papa Johns? I hope so, and we as fans can help us achieve that goal by turning up at Plough Lane on the 20th for the Wimbledon game and getting behind our team, after, of course, getting behind them in the three league games that come first.

14th September 2022

What to write about the most important of the least important things in my life? In a week when the nation has to come to terms with the ending of the second Elizabethan age and the beginning of the new Carolean age, this will be, for most of us, a time of united grief at the Queen's passing and hopefully will also be a time of celebration of a life spent in service for Her country and the Commonwealth of Nations.

It was inevitable, I suppose, that different organisations would deal with the situation in different ways, and I will respect the decision made by the Football authorities, without resorting to online abuse, but also with a feeling that they have come to the wrong choice of how to mark this historic and emotional time in our history.

Personally, I would have continued with fixtures last weekend, but would have moved them all to be at the same time, or as near to that as possible. This would have enabled the thousands of football supporters throughout the country to show their appreciation of a life well spent and to signal the commencement of the new age. A minute's silence followed by a minute's applause and finished off with the football family singing the new words to our National Anthem, would have been a great well-timed tribute to a woman of remarkable fortitude.

I guess we will have the chance to do this at a future match day, but if the football authorities think a suspension of fixtures is appropriate, wouldn't it have been better to provide their clubs with time to prepare for it. Clubs, up and down the country, will have planned for last weekend, purchased food, laid on staff and all the other necessities that go with a match day. Hotels and transport will have been booked for away teams, and all this in a time of rising costs and increasing austerity.

Hopefully charities will be able to benefit from perishable food items donated by clubs, which I think was the plan at The Broadfield, or perhaps the football authorities will foot the bill for their decision.

In case anyone thinks I am being disrespectful, then read the article again and hopefully you will see that I am as keen to mark Her Majesty's passing as anyone and celebrate her wonderful life.

Her life began in 1926, the same year as our own Stan Markham and the invention of television. Crawley FC, yet to add the suffix Town, were playing in the Mid Sussex League in front of the proverbial two men and a dog. She trained as a driver and mechanic during the war, whilst football at our level was suspended, and our lads, including Stan, went off to war. Since the second world war she has had to go through both bad and good times, much like the rest of us I suspect, but without doubt showed a fortitude of spirit that encompasses the meaning of our own motto, Noli Cedere, Never Give Up.

Her Majesty Queen Elizabeth II has passed, God Save the King

21ˢᵗ September 2022

I had written half of this article before the game on Saturday, and then Gary Smith goes and purloins my Four Ts tag line. I refer, of course, to the Tilley, Telford, Tsaroulla and Tom Nichols collaboration last Tuesday against Stockport County which brought us our first victory of the season.

Before I write about Saturday's defeat to Crewe Alexandra, I would like to write about the item which has dominated the news for a week and a half. The vast majority of people in this country, whether of a royalist or republican nature, have treated the passing of HM Queen Elizabeth II with the utmost respect, and we were given the chance to pay our respects as a club before the Stockport game. As always we did it properly and I was heartened to see the same respect shown at the vast majority of games throughout this country. Vast majority, though, means that some didn't, and without mentioning names I have to wonder at what goes through the minds of people when they decide to act in this way. What, for instance, makes a player in this country decide to not link arms with his team mates during the silence? What makes supporters of any home nationality, irrespective of the politics or ideology, show disrespect for anyone who has just died? Sadness is not compulsory, but surely respect should be.

Anyway, back to the football of the most importance to us. Following on from the first win in the league last Tuesday, Crawley Town were faced with what is always a difficult trip for us. Not in the journey, but in the game itself. Crewe always seem to beat us, even though I know we have recorded three victories against them, the last being at Broadfield in 2018, defeats at their hands are in double figures with four matches being drawn. Even the three nil home victory in 2018 saw Glenn Morris made Man of the Match in a game where Crewe outplayed us in all aspects, except where it counts. Saturday's match saw Rebecca Welch in charge of the game, the first time a female has refereed one of our matches, and overall seemed to have a good game according to Kevin Betsy, although, both he and Tom Nichols thought she should have issued a second yellow to their goal scorer, Baker-Richardson, importantly before he scored the winner. On the reverse side of the "What If "argument, if we had scored from just one of our very scarce chances, we would have got a result.

Last Tuesday, however, did see us take our chances and saw us gain that first league win of the season. taking us to five games unbeaten in all competitions. We didn't make it six in a row at Crewe, but I do find it hard to accept the logic of some fans that would have preferred us to have drawn both games, thus extending our run. The last time I looked, three points was worth more than two, although I do accept psychologically a defeat could set you back confidence wise.

AFC Wombles next, followed by Donny Rovers, both away, and a chance to start a new run of unbeaten matches??? Noli Cedere

28th September 2022

Before I talk about on the field expectations, actualities and where we go from here, I would like to express my gratitude to the majority of supporters who travelled to the impressive Plough Lane stadium last Tuesday. The majority of our fans, although frustrated with the manner of defeat, stuck behind the lads throughout although no doubt frustrated, as I am, at the way the season has begun. I would like to pick out five supporters, not by name, but they know who they are, for making sure I got there and back safely, as my days of making my own way to away games are sadly long gone. Unfortunately, for every person who sticks religiously to the "Town, Team, Together" mantra, there are a few who seem to want to criticise from the word go and spend most of their time looking toward the bench and offering advice, not in a constructive manner but with real venom and negativity. I won't harp on about this anymore as I would like to comment on an incident which ultimately cost us the game. Mazeed Ogungbo had the ball in our penalty area, right in front of my seat when he slipped on the turf, falling forward with his hand out stretched. I am not saying he didn't intentionally handle the ball, as he clearly did. However, in so doing he played the ball into the path of the Don's forward, who, seeing the referee wave play on, shot at goal from six yards out only to see Robson pull off a magnificent save. The referee then awarded the penalty, sent off Mazeed and Wimbledon went one up. Anything wrong with that? Well. I'm not sure. I thought that to be sent off for handball in the area you had to be preventing a goal scoring opportunity, whereas, in fact, Mazeed actually gave them the opportunity to score. Personally, I would rather he had hoofed the ball clear before he slipped over, but that's another discussion. We were punished twice for the one offence and this surely can't be right. Please discuss and let me know what you feel, with respect, of course.

And then we, the team that is, went to Doncaster and, after having a fair go for the first 60 minutes, capitulated in an inexcusable manner by losing four goals to one. Yes, the ref was from Yorkshire, yes, he did give Doncaster the softest of penalties when we were on top, but then we seemed to play with no cohesion and no real desire to get back in the game. Something needs to change, and quickly, if we are to climb even as far as mid table. Change of strategy, change of coach or both, but something needs to be done for the promise of aggressive, adaptable, attacking football to be realised. Hats off to those who travelled to either of this week's games, sandwiching another defeat for the three lions, and I hope I regret writing this just after watching the Donny game, and that we triumph in the Newtown Derby next week against someone who we all know quite well.

5th October 2022

What have Gareth Southgate and Kevin Betsy have in common? Well, they both have their supporters and they both have their denigrators, which, I suppose, makes football the game it is. Where everyone has an opinion on how games should be played, which seems to vary depending on what results are achieved. The thing they don't have in common, apart from the length of service, is how much time they have with their charges. To want to ditch GS with the World Cup barely two months away seems wrong to me, especially when we all know how England can play, as they showed in the second half against Germany last Monday. Writing this now, three hours before Crawley Town kick off in the New Town Derby, I want Kevin and our lads to show us what they can do against a team who are doing well this season under the tutelage of the man who was provided with the ammunition to get us into the league, Steve Evans. Read on for how I felt after the event.

Sunday Morning

Devastated, downhearted and absolutely confused about what should happen. In my opinion, you couldn't blame Saturday's defeat on the way we set up or how we played. In my opinion, we matched Steve's streetwise Stevenage all game and should have at least got a point. With Preston in attendance there will be a lot for him and WAGMI to ponder in the next month, but I am sure he will be gladdened by the imminent return to the matchday squad of George Francomb and Dion Conroy. Hopefully James

Balagizi will also be available after his international sojourn and Joel Lynch will continue in the side.

I listened to rumours yesterday about how Kevin and Dan were not "liked" by the "changing room" and then I listened to Joel Lynch and Kevin Betsy appear to contradict that. I would appeal here for fans not to get involved in third party Chinese whispers and remember, that in football, patience is the most important thing. (Credit to some big bloke who plays for Manchester City).

As previously stated, I am confused about how we get out of the situation we are in, but with returning experienced players I am hopeful for an upturn in our form sooner rather than later.

In 2020/2021 there was a team that made a slightly better start than us, picking up 10 points after eleven games, but had been knocked out of the EFL Cup and were halfway to exiting the Trophy as well. By halfway through the season, they had picked up a little but had still only achieved 30 points in 23 games. In the second half of the season, they won 49 points from 69 available and were promoted at the People's Pension Stadium. They are of course Bolton Wanderers. Now, in order to match their achievement, we must first of all win eight out of the next twelve games to achieve 30 points which would take us to the next transfer window. Dreaming? Probably, but I would rather that than hurl real venomous abuse at people who they object to.

PS 174 people unable to return home after a football match in Indonesia. Perspective everyone.

12th October 2022

For our second match running at Blundell Park, albeit two years apart, we were faced by an ex Red Devil. This time, it was Crawley lad Jordan Maguire-Drew, whereas last time it was Philipe Morais.

For our second match running at Blundell Park, albeit two years apart, we couldn't defend a free kick. Although this year it was certainly a lot better free kick than that scored by Morais in our last encounter. Only being able to listen to it on Ifollow, I was not confident, because of our poor record this year in defending against them, as I think that makes it four out of five that we have not defended against. What the reason is, I don't know. Not lining the wall up correctly, not positioning yourself properly or just incredibly bad luck. Take your pick.

I could ramble on about the referee and the linesman appearing to change their mind about the validity of Dom Telford's goal just before half time, but that would be hiding from the realisation that something needed to be done, if we are to turn our fortunes around before it's too late.

To add insult to injury, I thought we had equalised on 8 minutes when I saw Kwesi Appiah had scored on the Sky programme, but then I remembered that our leading scorer from last season was out on loan in deepest Essex.

One thing is for sure, until the end of the season we can't go any lower than we already are, and what is needed now is real commitment from all associated with the Club that we all want to be successful.

I know for a fact that our American owners are as down, as the staunchest of our supporters, about the position we find ourselves in, not because I heard it from a mate, who heard it from someone who overheard somebody chatting about it in the barbers, but because I talked to Preston myself on Friday at the Foundation run Extra Time Hub, and as I write this, whilst watching Arsenal V Liverpool on my tablet, he has shown his understanding of our plight by severing our links with Kevin Betsy and Dan Micciche.

Lewis Young is to serve as interim manager I believe, as he did last season. But my choice as interim would have been Tony Craig, that is assuming he would want to do it. What we must do now, is be positive and if we don't win Saturday, for whatever reason, we must get behind the team selected. One question that does need answering, is what will be the status of loan players, both ours out with other clubs and the likes of Fellows and Balagizi who were trusted to us because of Kevin and Dan.

Personally, I hope James Balagizi can come back from Liverpool quickly and fully fit. I hope that Dom Telford scores a hat trick against his old club next week and above all else, I hope that our season kick starts soon and we maintain our Football League status. NC TTT SOES

Looking forward to the bounce.

19th October 2022

Well, what to say about football, in general, and Crawley Town specifically. Artell, Robinson, Ferguson, Woodman are all in the bookies lists, as is Lewis Young, but not all of them are in the thinking of Preston Johnson and Wagmi United.

At the moment Lewis is in charge, and judging by Saturday, if nothing else, he deserves the full support of everyone involved with CTFC whilst he is charge. Whether it be for the short term or the longer haul. The players certainly showed their support for him, not only in the way they played, with a new found enthusiasm and desire, but also in the way they celebrated the first goal with him at the dugout. Newport had their chances to prolong our agony, but didn't take them, and we took two of ours exquisitely to put a smile back on the 2600 home supporters in attendance, in a crowd of just over 2800. Newport probably scored the goal of the game, but one of the highlights for me was seeing Ashley Nadesan, after being substituted, vigorously applauding an agricultural clearance from one of our defenders in the last six minutes of 97 played. Now, that's what you call playing it out from the back, League 2 style.

Whether Kevin and Dan would have won that game is irrelevant. However, I would like to say that I feel it a real shame that they weren't successful but also that we had reached the time for something to change.

Next up, although it's before this will be published, is our home game with Aston Villa U 21 side in the Papa John's trophy. I will be there, even though I don't believe that they should be playing in the competition, because I will be supporting my team. Just in case you aren't aware, if we win outright on Tuesday, without the need for penalties we will finish the group stage on 5 points, with Wimbledon and Portsmouth, to play each other on November 1st on 6 and 4 points respectively, after their first two games. This means that we will all need to be Plastics on their match day. An outright win for AFC will send us through, although I'm not sure what will happen if Pompey are defeated on penalties. Anyway, first things first, a win against Villa is an absolute necessity.

Next Saturday, we entertain the Stags of Mansfield Town in the League, followed by Colchester United and Bradford City away. As Phil Townsend reminded me on Saturday, we always play better against teams above us in the league, so will this urban myth be proved right over the next two weeks, and if so, is there any rush to appoint a new manager?

Coming back down to earth, I would be pleased with five points from those three games and absolutely ecstatic with a maximum nine. Follow that with qualification in the PJT on November 1st, (thanks to AFC, I hope) an FA CUP victory on the fifth and the beating of Burnley on the 8th then perhaps we can put the past behind us.

26th October 2022

Before we look at on the field matters, I thought I would write about the financial crisis from a football clubs' point of view. Some non-league clubs are talking about the possibility of not being able to survive until the end of the season because of rising costs, such as floodlights, transport to away matches and catering supplies, which in some instances is made even worse by falling gates. Our opponents on Saturday had even brought forward their kick off time last week to avoid using their floodlights, so it would appear that financial worries are abound, even in league football. We appear to be lucky, , as our attendances are actually showing signs of increasing from last year's league average of 2293. With seven matches played at home, our average is currently showing a 30% increase to 2975, and all this with the backdrop of our poor, results wise, start to the season. However, before we start thinking we have an increase in income we have to remember the reduction in attendance costs introduced by our owners, Wagmi United. This virtually means that the income coming in through the gate is virtually the same as last season, whilst the costs of energy, transport and supplies have all gone up. The message I'm trying to get across, is that our team, our club, need all the support we can give them at the moment just to break even, let alone to get them up the league. And now, as in all good news broadcasts, here is the Football news.

It appears that we may have turned the corner without having another immediately in sight. Three wins on the bounce, all at home, have lightened the mood considerably amongst the fans, and have, I believe, taken the pressure off Wagmi United to make a knee jerk appointment for the post of manager. Lewis Young obviously has the respect of all under his charge, and whilst some fans might say he doesn't have enough contacts to be successful, surely that is what the Director of Football is for. I personally would like to see him left in charge for the foreseeable future and, even if he doesn't eventually secure the permanent position, kept on as a first team coach. His love and dedication for Crawley Town is there for all to see. In true Clough fashion, Nigel gave no credit to Crawley for the victory on Saturday, rather seeking to blame his defence for being "uncharacteristic" in gifting us our goals, and his forward line for being profligate with their shooting. I, however, would like to pay credit to the Stags for their resilience in putting the result in doubt at half time but, most importantly, want to sing the praises of Nadders and Super Tom for showing even more resilience in not giving in after the Stags had levelled. The winning goal, from the outside of the boot Tom Nichols pass, through the shrugging off of the Mansfield defender to the exquisite finish gives me more than just hope for Tuesday, it gives me an expectation. Fingers crossed it's four in a row by the time you read this.

2nd November 2022

Well, I said two weeks ago " I would be pleased with five from those three Games (MansField, Colchester and Bradford) and absolutely ecstatic with a maximum nine". Actually, I'll rephrase that and say I am absolutely ecstatic with the five gained, coming as they did with the victory against Villa U21s in the Papa John's Trophy just before them.

The next week sees us trying to progress in three cup competitions, albeit with the first game not actually involving us. That is, of course, the Portsmouth v AFC Wimbledon Papa John's game. We want, ironically, for our dear friends from Plough Lane to win. An outright win in the ninety minutes would see us qualify in second place, one point ahead of Pompey. A win on penalties, for the Wombles, gives the Hampshire side the same number of points as us, which, unfortunately, will put them through. This is because the rules state that if two teams are level on points the decision as to who progresses will be made on Goal difference in the first instance, goals scored secondly and then number of wins in normal time. The last deciding factor would be the head-to-head result of the two teams involved. Come on you plastics, beat them outright........please.

Anyway, as there is nothing we can do about that conundrum, so no need to worry about it, let's get back to our performances in the League and the other two cup matches we can do something about. A great point at the University of Bradford Stadium, saw us record our seventh point against them on their own pitch in the last three seasons. Once again everybody in my flats must have known we had equalised, by the loudness of my "Get In" when James Tilley hit that superb free kick, just five minutes after the Bantams had taken the lead. In my opinion, with my optimistic glasses on, it was a great point gained, in front of over 17000 hostile Yorkshire men, women, boys and girls and anybody else who was supporting the claret and amber side. Hats off to our away support, magnificent as always.

Looking back at the trip to Essex, I think, in time, we will see that as another valuable point gained rather than as two lost. The question I would like answered, would be if Kwesi had been fit, would he have been allowed to play against us. I thought, perhaps incorrectly, that loan players were not allowed to play against their parent clubs, but Chucky played against Villa for us and Gary Smith, in his commentary last Tuesday hinted that Kwesi had stated he would have been available for selection if he had been fit.

Clarification please, before we face Gillingham on the 22nd November and the Cat prevents us from scoring.

The players will now get a week of training to prepare them for the FA Cup game, against Accrington Stanley, followed by the trip to Turf Moor to face an in-form Burnley. I hope, that Lewis picks his strongest team for both games as I really think we could progress in both competitions, but as said previously, I am forever an optimist.

9th November 2022

As I awake and look around me, at the four beige walls that surround me, actually they're more magnolia, and they certainly aren't as bleak as those sung about by Tom Jones, being covered with Red Devils, Three Lions and general Crawley miscellanea, I am doing two of my most favourite things, whilst contemplating a third.

Favourite thing number one, writing, favourite thing number two, watching cricket (England V Sri Lanka) and of course, number three, thinking about FA Cup glory for my beloved Red Devils this afternoon against Accrington Stanley and hopefully beyond.

Neither Accrington nor Crawley have ever played at Wembley Stadium, although we have been there, back in 2011, when we picked up the giantkillers award before the Manchester City v Stoke City FA Cup final and the Oaks School, representing Crawley Town, did play there before the 2015 League 1 Play Off Final. Hang on a moment whilst I stop clutching my straw, but I would like to hear "Abide with me" whilst watching the Town, before I must explain to St Peter why we are the Red Devils.

And then I watched a game where we never really got going, apart from when the Accy defender provided the perfect headed pass for Jake Hessenethaler to equalise, and lost by four goals to one in a most uncharacteristic manner. The reaction from the crowd was encouraging, as most applauded the efforts of the team and Lewis Young at the final whistle and left the ground experiencing disappointment which will only last until the next victory.

Five minutes was the time taken for someone to say, "That's the distraction out of the way, we can now concentrate on the league!" and that seemed to open the floodgates for other comments about the future of Lewis Young, whether the Sidemen would have made a difference (tongue in cheek) and where our defence was when the second and third goals were scored and where the assistant ref was for the first and fourth goals. From behind the goal, they appeared to be offside, but I fully accept the assistant ref was in a better position to judge, only I don't believe he was as in both instances he appeared to be five yards behind the play.

Count to ten and breathe and on to the next match which could either end in glory or see us go out of three cups in a week. The first being due to AFC Wombles letting us down last Tuesday, the second being due to Saturday's defeat and the third????? Well, Burnley themselves suffered a loss by three goals, going down five two against Sheffield United, and next Saturday they face their close rivals, Blackburn Rovers. Close geographically and in terms of the league. Burnley top on 38 points and Rovers second on 36. This may mean an "understrength" Burnley team taking the field against Crawley, but I'm sure whoever dons the claret and blue on Tuesday will provide an effort that will need to be matched by a fighting, resilient approach from the boys wearing whatever colour we play in.

Of course, if you're reading this on Wednesday morning, you will know the result, and whatever it is I hope you will continue supporting the Red Devils..

16th November 2022

Two-part article this week, starting with our third cup exit in a week. Sounds awful, doesn't it? However, the third exit was one that, for me, left me feeling nothing but pride for all the players, Lewis Young and the majority of our supporters. I travelled up to Burnley, past ecological protestors and through horrendous weather, with six stalwart Crawley supporters, and after dinner ended up at Burnley Cricket Club, where Jimmy Anderson started his cricketing career. Packed mostly with Crawley supporters we waited anxiously for the team to be announced. and I was surprised, like anyone, to see who was playing and who was on the bench, but unlike some fans I was prepared to let them take the field before passing judgement.

Others, unfortunately, were not prepared to be so generous. "That team is a disgrace"," Lewis picked it to please the owners", "Wagmi team" blah, blah, blah.

On entering Turf Moor though, I was pleased to see and hear that the majority of the 311 travelling Reds fans were prepared to support from the start and the chanting never stopped throughout the entire match, albeit that some of it, although supporting Crawley, was inappropriate and excluded a large section of our support. There was also a chant insinuating that more people in Burnley were on benefits than in Crawley, whereas a check of the facts shows it to be the other way round. Also, why travel to support your team if you're going to spend most of the game watching and goading the opposition supporters rather than watching the action on the pitch.

I only hope that the pre match doom sayers had noticed that the disgrace of a team had got so close to holding out against top of the Championship, Burnley and perhaps our best result ever.

Part two.

Following the route one goal, scored by Telford and assisted by Balcombe, on Tuesday, we scored a route three effort on Saturday with Tsaroulla and Nadesan joining in the move. Once again Ellery started the move by finding Nick on the left, who in turn found Dom who crossed low and hard for Nads to smash it into the net. After that, both teams were mainly "agricultural" in their approach with me, and many others having stiff necks as a result. A hard-fought victory was won against a team in fourth position in the league and which extends our unbeaten league run to five. Sutton are now just two points ahead of us and we have a game in hand, which is against Gillingham on the 22nd of November.

Things are generally on the up with results going our way, the fan zone nearing completion and the partnership with Southwater providing us grass pitch training facilities, for which Ben, at Complete Turf Care, deserves a lot of credit.

The Sussex Senior Cup, which I would love us to win, must surely give all our fringe players a chance to shine. If we win against old foes Hastings United that would be great, but I have come round to thinking it is more valuable for bringing our young players experience than for the kudos it would give the club. What do you think?

23rd November 2022

Saturday evening ten past five and absolutely gutted. Gutted for Lewis Young, gutted for the team who fought so valiantly after Ludo's dismissal on 39 minutes and gutted for all Crawley Town fans, whether they were at Poundland, watching it at home, listening to it whilst cruising to New York or whilst recovering in hospital.

I would have been pleased with a draw before the game, ecstatic at half time and over the moon at the end of the game, but you just knew it wasn't going to be our day when Ashley Nadesan's curling shot, in injury time, just failed to curl enough to end up in the top corner of the Saddlers net.

The run has come to an end, but there is nothing to stop a new one from starting (yesterday) against Gillingham and then with two more home games to come over the next two and a half weeks.

I hope "Town Team Together" stay together over this period, as the worst thing that could happen now would be for negativity to creep back into the club.

As for the Sussex Senior Cup defeat at Hastings, I have to admit that for once, I was not devastated with the loss as I would have been in the past. Memories of trips to the Pilot Field are many for those who are as old as me, and not just for the football played. Indeed, I remember one season when three matches were called off there, one just as we turned up, before the fourth finally allowed the contest to come to a conclusion. John Barnett or Mick Fox will probably correct my recall and come up with dates and the result.

Good things are happening at our club at the moment, including the construction of the fan zone outside Redz and the establishing of a partnership with Southwater FC to enable our players to train on grass. I, for one, will be at the fan zone for the England group games, and hopefully beyond, and will be praying that the Three Lions finish top of group B, to avoid having to move the Swindon home game on the 3rd December.

Going back to the Walsall game, I think Ellery Balcombe had an outstanding game for Crawley, and if anybody didn't deserve to be on a losing side it was him. I am not sure about the sending off, but if it had been their Centre half, I don't think I would have objected. The referee, for once, didn't affect the result in my opinion but he did annoy me slightly at one point, when he was hit by the ball and waved play on.

I am sure Lewis, and the lads would have been hurting on the journey home from the Midlands, as would all the supporters, but it will all be forgotten if, by the time you read this we have started another three-match winning streak, which, come December 9th, will make it six home victories on the trot.

Noli Cedere

30th November 2022

The important thing to take from Tuesday's game against Gillingham, is that we didn't lose. Yes, we should be aiming to win games against teams at the bottom of the table, but at least the gap between us and them has been maintained. The day before the Gills game, I spent two and a half hours in the company of anglophile Crawley Town fans in the Redz bar. The atmosphere was good and optimistic, following the professional six two demolition of the "mighty" Iran, and although the new fans zone wasn't needed for that match, it certainly was for the USA game.

Unfortunately, the ITV cameras in Redz bar didn't get a chance to show Crawley fans celebrating an England win, as at times it seemed we were watching a rerun of the Crawley V Gillingham game. Once again, I must say, at least we (England) didn't lose.

The result of the upcoming game on Tuesday (last night if you're reading this how it should be read, on paper) against Wales could now affect our (Crawley Town) game against Swindon on the 3rd December. England must win to guarantee playing the Round of 16 game on Sunday 4th December. A draw would also do it if Iran draw against USA, but if either of them win........aaargh. Forget the what ifs, I'm not even going to look at Wales beating us by four goals, for that won't (hasn't) happen (happened). If England finish second in the group our next match would be at 3pm on the 3rd December, when Crawley are due to face Swindon. Anyone fancy a lunch time kick off?

A second-place finish in Group B or even worse, an exit from the World Cup, would be sure to ignite calls for the dismissal of Crawley boy Gareth Southgate, and whilst I am writing this article the news is out that Wagmi have made a managerial decision for Crawley Town, with Lewis Young leaving the club with immediate effect, to be replaced by Matthew Etherington with Simon Davies as his assistant. The club website states that Etherington and Davies come from managing the Peterborough U23 side, whereas in fact they were Posh's U21 bosses as Peterborough hasn't got an U23 side.

Preston says that Etherington and Davies are data driven, and by that I presume he means player data, as if you compare the team data of Lewis Young in charge at Crawley with that of the Posh duo, Lewis comes out on top by about 14%. Aristotle, that well known Greek philosopher and football fan, once said "The whole is greater than the individual parts" which fits in well with it being a team sport.

Having said that, both Matt Etherington and Simon Davies deserve to be treated with respect and judged on their performance at Crawley Town. Let's hope they continue the upturn in our fortune started by Lewis Young.

Earlier in the day, last Tuesday, I had the immense privilege of talking with Lewis about his life and was impressed with the way he spoke candidly about personal issues and football. He may have come from Stevenage, but Crawley flowed through his blood. Lewis Young, you will be missed.

7th December 2022

Part 1

I should have been getting up this morning (Sunday)full of elation over yesterday's fantastic victory giving way to being full of expectation for our game next week, and of course for the England v Senegal clash this evening.

However, the expectation is being edged out of my brain by a feeling of anxiety about the future of who, for me, is the best current Red Devil, Tom Nichols. Sam Morton has reported "The manager revealed that the forward (super Tommy Nichols) wasn't injured and the decision to leave him "was out of my hands". Sam said "He didn't want to elaborate".

There have been rumours, during the past week, of Bradford City wanting both Tom and Nadders which I find hard to believe or accept, them being one of our competitors. I was fairly calm about this as the same source said that he (Tom) had signed for Mansfield during the summer. Another rumour linked him with Sunderland, but that appears to be a year old, whilst yet another is circulating that Tom is being disciplined for something he has said about Lewis Young's departure. I can categorically say that isn't the case, but I'm sure all will be revealed soon, and if it is that Tom is leaving, I hope it is to at least a League 1 club and would like to thanks him for what he has done for our club.

Anyway, back to the football. To a man, the players did us proud yesterday and stopped Swindon from getting any shots on target enabling us to get our third clean sheet in a row at home, and the return of James Balagizi certainly made us more potent going forward. The bench also contributed to our success, in Tilley and Oteh providing refreshed energy when it was needed, culminating in Aramide chasing down their keeper and forcing him to feed Jack Powell with the ball, only to see him lob it back over his head from fully 45 yards into an empty net.

A great afternoon, made even better by most of the teams below us dropping points.

Part two

Another evening spent in the company of both blood and football families and a great performance by the three lions, which means another evening at Redz next Saturday to watch us destroy France, Mbappe and all. I will continue dreaming that it's coming home for Christmas until someone proves otherwise. I am going for a four-nil win for Crawley on Saturday and a tight two nil win for England over France. I think that the last time England beat France by that score in a World Cup finals, we went on to win the Jules Rimet Trophy.

Here's hoping for both these dreams to come true.

14th December 2022

I have just watched Matty Etherington's summing up of the Hartlepool game played in freezing temperatures, and he didn't appear to be very happy with the effort put in by the team selected to face a team, that were not only bottom of the division but had lost five nil at home in their last match.

I am not one to get on a manager's back after just two games in charge, as I think we should first look at the team selected and acknowledge the fact that it would not have been the manager's first choice.

There was no Francomb, Francilette, Jenks, Oteh, Fellows or Robson available for selection because of injury or sickness, which under other regimes might have meant not covering the pitch the day before in order that the game would be postponed. On top of that, in the first fifteen minutes we lost the services of Ashley Nadesan and Joel Lynch through muscle injuries, and the script for the night was set. Harry Ransom, coming on for Lynch, played well I thought, but for Crawley to have only one effort on target, and that from a James Tilley header, begs the question that all Crawley fans want answered.

What is the reason for Tom Nichols absence? Surely, we are not letting his "new" club dictate to us that he can't play until the window opens, are we? Perhaps if he was Premier League or Championship bound for a huge fee, that might, just, be understandable. However, the clubs being rumoured to be in the frame are mostly League two clubs, and ones that we should not sell any of our players to, or, even for that matter, loan out to.

Honesty and transparency are what we were promised by WAGMI, so here's a question for our owners. Is Matty Etherington allowed to select the team based on his and Simon Davies' judgement of the squad, as surely Tom would be in any first team at the Broadfield Stadium, whether the rest of the squad were fit or not?

On a ranking these are the most important things in my life.

Family, Health, Crawley Town, England, Everything Else

Suddenly, England, after the Crawley game, were at the top of my ranking because of the World Cup. I, along with a Redz bar and a marquee full of eager, anticipatory three lions' supporters hoped above everything that this year would be our year. Sadly, it wasn't to be, as the usually dependable Harry Kane missed his second spot kick and the older members of those watching thought back to all those "so nearly" times that had gone before. Younger members of the audience learning another valuable lesson in what it means to support your team with all your heart.

In my opinion, the better team on the night lost, not because of a lack of effort or skill, dubious decisions or a flash of oppositional brilliance, but simply because in football those sorts of things happen.

Now, cheer me up someone, please. Tell me Super Tom has signed a new contract.

21st December2022

What to write about, when no real football is being played. Only joking, as I am writing this after having witnessed a pulsating World Cup Final between Argentina and France. I wanted France to win by two clear goals so I could say, avec ma langue fermement dans ma joue, that we were better than the Argentinians. Never mind, there's always next time.

That wish to see France win was coupled with a desire to see Mbappe miss a penalty so Harry Kane could have a laugh at him. Once again though, that wasn't to be.

Last Friday, after having eaten something that didn't agree with me, I was forced to miss three Christmas events so that I could take part in the Armitage Shanks Handicap, and I was also disappointed to see our game had been postponed at Tranmere.

It seems their grounds man had misplaced their covers and thus the game was frozen off.

That doesn't leave much else to talk about, Crawley Town wise, as we are still not permitted to know what is happening with Tom Nichols. As it seems likely that he is leaving when the January transfer window opens, it would have been good to have had the opportunity to have seen him play one more time for Crawley Town, especially as it would have been against Sutton United in a boxing Day Derby match.

Of course, I could be, and I hope I will be, proved wrong in the club he has been linked with, but if that's the case why not tell us now? A fans' forum is what is needed in my opinion, with owners, Director of football, manager and players being present, so that supporters can at least be reassured as to why we are letting our best player leave, especially to one of our nearest competitors.

Before I ruin everyone's Christmas, I feel I should mention that Sutton United, in one of just two EFL League 2 games played on Saturday, lost two nil putting them just five points ahead of us with having played one game more. Hopefully, the extended break, caused by the Tranmere postponement, will give Matty and the team a chance for injuries and sicknesses to heal and be cured, so that we can start to close the gap between us and them.

I hope that all Red Devil fans and those who you love and cherish have a happy and healthy Christmas and a New Year which sees us looking forward and upwards with renewed optimism, rather than downwards with feelings of despair and distrust. Town, Team, Together

28th December 2022

Hi everyone. This is my last article of 2022, and as it is being written before Christmas to meet the Observer deadline of the 23rd of December, it does not include any details about the fantastic four nil home victory over Sutton United, which is yet to be played. Neither does it include details on what Paul Tarran has spent his winnings on from his fortnightly bets on four nil home wins. Wouldn't it be great if that came true?

So, with no Crawley Town football to speak of this week, except for a two one win at West Ham's training ground against their U21 side, I thought it would be useful to look at how our beloved team has performed throughout 2022.

In January, under John Yems, we took nine points out of a possible eighteen and, in February, this sort of form was repeated when we took another eight points out of fifteen. Unfortunately, March wasn't as profitable, eight from twenty-four, but the John Yems era came to an end in April with nine points from twelve, before Lewis Young took over with just one point from the last nine available.

This gave John Yems an almost 50% success rate in terms of League points gained, thirty-four from sixty-nine (69) available, which, if what occurred next hadn't happened, would almost certainly have meant him still being in charge until the end of last season at least.

Then came the Betsy era, which promised so much but delivered so little, and despite of beating Premier League Fulham in the Carabao Cup, he departed the club on the 9th of October, after a three nil away defeat to Grimsby Town, and having secured just six points from the thirty-nine available.

Lewis Young, then took up the reins, the tiller, the steering wheel (insert your favourite cliché here) for the next seven games, and, during his time at the helm, saw the team collect twelve points from twenty-one, put up a spirited performance away at Burnley but crash out of the FA Cup against Accrington Stanley. Up until the introduction of Matty Etherington and Simon Davies as our 4th or 5th management team of the year, Lewis was our most successful manager in terms of league points won, with a 57% success rate, against John's 49% and Kevin's 15%. Before anyone disputes Lewis' figure, I haven't included the three games at the end of last season, which, if included, would take his figures down to 42%.

Where are we now? Well, we have a manager who has overseen just two games with a 50% success rate, which could be either 66% or 33% by the time you read this. Not sufficient data, I hear you shout, and you're absolutely right, but at some point, we must give a manager time to get things right and the ability to always pick his best team available, and not allow other clubs to influence our team selection.

In closing, I hope you have had a great Christmas and that the rest of the season sees Matty Etherington's Red Devils maintain a minimum of a 66% success rate, which would mean us finishing on at least 71 points.

Is that Santa's sleigh bells I can hear?

4th January 2023

Well, having fantasized about beating Sutton United four nil I guess it's time to wake up and smell the coffee. Having said that, as there are too many unresolved variables, perhaps I shouldn't bother writing anymore. Yes, I am down about my football club at the moment. which as everybody should know by now is a rare occurrence, but until our owners are open and honest as to why we can't pick our best team, then down is where I shall remain.

Having listened to the after-match views of Matty Etherington and George Francomb post Boxing Day, I would like to know whether their wish for some new faces to supplement the side will be realised by our owners, especially as we have transferred our talisman, Tom Nichols. Not only transferring him, but to a team who we are in direct competition with. No matter what the owners come up with as an explanation for Tom's omission from our squad and his eventual departure, I find it hard to accept that he has gone to a club bottom of the division that we are fighting to stay in ourselves.

Football itself seems to be taking a back seat at the moment, with so much going on in the background at the club. To be looking for our fourth management regime of the season less than halfway into the season must, I feel, indicate that all is not right within the House of Wagmi.

I don't blame Matty Etherington and Simon Davies for departing the club, as it seems to me that with the transfer window due to open soon, they have probably been told there is no budget to strengthen the current squad.

Praying that this is not the case, but until we see evidence to the contrary from our "frank and open" owners what else are we supposed to believe. Matty Etherington was possibly promised something that has not materialised, and probably left out of the decision to let Tom Nichols depart. Unless they make a statement as to the reasons for their departures, I fear we will never know the truth of either matter.

Where does all this leave the people who matter the most, the players, supporters and staff? Initially facing ridicule from other clubs in our league, but I would ask all our fans to back the players as they always do, with spirit, emotion and heart. This is the only way we will get through this nadir in our history, that and the appointment of a manager with League 2 experience prepared for a fight.

Meanwhile, in what really counts, the football, we went down to Stevenage by three goals to one, with stalwarts Francomb, Hessenthaler and Craig not in the squad and then followed that up with a two all draw away to Newport County. To be fair, we would probably have lost to Stevenage with the missing trio on the pitch, but the question must be asked, would they have got us over the line against County. At two nil up with just ten minutes to play, would the more experienced heads have seen us through.

Never mind, just to show how statistics and data should be treated with care, we are currently undefeated in 2023.

11ᵗʰ January 2023

The sorry saga, that came to light just as Wagmi bought our club, now seems to have reached some sort of conclusion, at least, according to the FA. John Yems may think otherwise, but, as someone who got on well with him, I think it is now time for us all to move on, club, supporters (on both sides of the argument), players, staff and JY himself.

We have other concerns now to put to rest, and it is with great sorrow that I understand that some of our fans seem to think it's alright to wish ill, or worse, on people and accuse them of all sorts of vile and insidious behaviour, just because they disagree with them.

Meanwhile, the membership of the CTSA, the supporter's representative body, has increased by over 2000% to a number now pushing 500 members, all with full voting rights, when it comes to deciding what the position should be as regards the multitude of issues that need addressing with WAGMI as an urgent necessity, if we are to avoid relegation or even worse.

Reuben Watt (interim chair}, Sam Jordan and Matt Cowdrey (CTSA member on Board of CTFC) have met with Preston Johnson, post his broadcast address to the fans, to discuss issues across the full spectrum of the club, including Governance structure, Finances, playing concerns, Media and Communications and how we can all get together to ensure our club goes forward and upwards.

I have no doubt that by the time you read this, a record of what was discussed will have been published on the CTSA website and that, hopefully, it will have addressed some, if not all, of our concerns. Having spoken to Preston myself last Friday, whilst watching walking football, I got the impression that he was well aware of the concerns we all share. That appeared to be the case when he issued his statement from the changing rooms on Saturday, and one can only hope that he shares the late Giannluca Vialli's philosophy that you either win or learn.

He certainly did not come across as an authoritarian figure hell bent on driving us into the ground, but as someone who still believes in the journey we are all on. Having said that, only time will tell and on Saturday we face a team, in Doncaster Rovers, who want to get back into League one at the first attempt and thus will provide a stern test of our resolve. I will be there, in Redz before the game and in my usual spot on the Winfield terrace during the game, supporting the players who wear the red of Crawley Town. I would ask that you consider doing the same, and leave any form of demonstration against our owners, if you still feel it necessary, till after the game. Who knows, I may even join you if the outcome of the meeting between Preston and the CTSA hasn't provided us with answers to our concerns that we can all live with. Noli Cedere, Noli Semper Cedere, Town, Team, Together.

16th January 2023

Another new era, or just the same old, same old? Well, we will all have to wait a little longer to see, following the postponement of the Doncaster Rovers match because of a waterlogged pitch. Scott Lindsay's interview and the CTSA meeting with Preston Johnson last Sunday have shed some light on the questions asked and the concerns held by many supporters without really allaying all the worries that we, as fans, might have. I do take heart however, in witnessing George Francomb, Jake Hessenthaler and Ashley Nadesan taking part in training and hopefully the extra week off will be used by all to prove their rightful places in the match day squad.

The extra week will also give Scott and Jamie Day (his assistant) time to further evaluate the squad and use the last two weeks of the transfer window effectively as we must face facts that we are in a relegation battle that must be addressed by all who love our club. Owners, Management, Players and Supporters.

With Rochdale at home to Colchester , Gillingham facing Hartlepool and Harrogate entertaining Stevenage we won't lose much ground today on those around us. Super Tom puts Gillingham ahead just before half time, wouldn't you just know it, but the Gills remain bottom despite adding another goal to beat the monkey hangers two nil.

Rochdale went down two one to Colchester, Harrogate earned a creditable one one draw at home to Stevenage whilst the next week's opponents for Crawley, Sutton United, lost to Salford City.

Looking at the league table the bottom seven are four points adrift from Crewe Alexandra in 17th place and our mini league looks like this

Position	Team	Played	Goal difference	Points
18	Newport County	26	-6	26
19	Colchester United	26	-7	26
20	Harrogate Town	25	-8	24
21	Crawley Town	24	-13	22
22	Rochdale	26	-17	20
23	Hartlepool United	25	-23	19
24	Gillingham	24	-19	17

The next four games are absolutely critical for us, if we are to avoid relegation, as we are away to Sutton United, home to Salford City and Grimsby Town then away to Gillingham. We have played the least number of games along with Gillingham, but you do have to make the most of the games in hand to take advantage of that position. If we did win the games in hand over Harrogate, Colchester and Newport we would go above them, but with Tom Nichols on their side, Gillingham might also start to make ground on those above them. Today was the first time they had scored more than one goal in a game this season, but we all know what Tom is capable of.

During the space of our four games there are quite a few games involving bottom 7 v bottom 7 but all we can do is to plan for our performances and our results, knowing that if we get them right it won't matter what the other teams do.

Keep the faith and Noli Semper Cedere

25th January 2023

In a week when Ellery Balcombe and James Ballagizi went back to their parent clubs for different reasons, we faced the possibility of playing Sutton United away with just Corey Addai to play in goal and no substitute keeper, David Robson having been called back to Hull the week previously. I have no doubt Corey would have given his all for the cause and, just as we set off for Gander Green Lane, we heard rumours that we had a keeper on the bench from Dulwich Hamlet but that a first-choice keeper is likely to be confirmed on Monday.

Just as the train pulled in to Salfords the news came through that the pitch at Sutton had been declared unplayable at an 11am inspection and thus we jumped off at Redhill, caught the next train back and settled for lunch in the Snooty Fox, whilst watching the Liverpool v Chelsea game. The football was so riveting that we were able to talk about Crawley Town's future without really being distracted.

With a home game scheduled for Tuesday, provided Brighton let us keep the heated cover for two more days (in situ because of Brighton Women hosting Arsenal Women), it should give us the opportunity to, hopefully, make up some ground on those around us. Whilst we should have been playing Sutton, Tom Nichols added to his goal tally in helping the Gills gain a two nil away win over Colchester and Hartlepool defeated nine-man Rochdale by the same score, but this time at home. This means, that as of 5pm on Saturday, Hartlepool are now on the same number of points as us, but having played two games more, and that Gillingham have now moved off the bottom on goal difference, with Rochdale taking their place, having played two games more. We have one game in hand on the Kentish team, and three over Rochdale. We also have games in hand over Newport, Colchester and Harrogate which, if we won them (I know, red coloured specs and all that) would see us climb almost to a respectable 18th.

What do we need to do to achieve these victories? Well, firstly we need to make, in my opinion, three or four quality signings, starting with that goalkeeper, or make sure Scott Lindsay can select from our entire squad. What would also be good would-be Hartlepool losing away to Carlisle when we play Grimsby, and for Salford to win at Colchester on the same night. As supporters we can do nothing about those results, but we can affect whoever puts on the red shirt by getting behind the players from minute one to whenever the referee wants to call time.

With five of the bottom nine to play at home, Crewe, Colchester, Harrogate and Rochdale coming up after Grimsby, our future is firmly in the hands, or should it be feet, of our players, so instead of waiting for them to lift us, the fans, why don't we try and lift them from the start and see where that takes us. Oh, just one other thing, why not delay your half time drink to half time? It might just make all the difference.

1ˢᵗ February 2023

A week in the life of a septuagenarian, Red Devil supporting, ginger gone grey haired, Parkinson's sufferer who desperately wants to see us in League 2 next season.

No news is good news, or so they say, but it would be good to see some action in the transfer market during the January window. I do get Preston's point about Scott having to assess his current squad before strengthening but all we have seen so far is some pruning, which I also accept was inevitable. We are in urgent need of another goalkeeper, and at the moment Matt Harrold or Ian Payne would do. But wait, we have signed Roshan Greensall after having let him go at the end of his previous contract. Good luck Roshan, but why did we not just extend his previous contract?

On top of that, we also need someone who is taller than Tom Nichols up front, as I think we would all agree his size let him down where it matters. What's that? He scored for the Gills with his head? Surely it must have been a low cross, wink wink.

We did get some good news on Tuesday night, in that our postponed game against Grimsby maintains our unbeaten start in this calendar year, and, less sarcastically, in Colchester dropping 2 points and Hartlepool dropping all three against Salford and Carlisle respectively. These results putting Crawley five points behind the Essex side and two behind the Monkey hangers with four and three games in hand respectively.

Rumours still circulating prior to the game against Salford City suggested that we will be signing another keeper and one other player before the deadline and that the trio of Francomb, Craig and Hessenthaler have played their last games for the club. All, hopefully, will be explained when the window has closed, but, however sad we may feel at the departure of any players, it is now time to look forward and support the lads who are still wearing the shirt.

The game itself saw Corey Addai come in in goal, replacing Ellery Balcombe, who on his debut for Bristol Rovers conceded five at Morecambe, and also saw the inclusion of Rafiq Khaleel for his full League debut and the return of Dion Conroy after a long injury setback. Right from the start it was apparent that the mood was different in the way we played with intensity and aggression. This transmitted to the crowd, a very few of which had come with homemade "Wagmi Out" posters, and very soon Crawley were doing what they always do against Salford at home, winning.

Two goals in the first half, both headers from Jack Powell corners, scored by Dom Telford and Dion Conroy, had ignited the atmosphere in the stadium and the talk was about football instead of owners and inquiries. The second half, at least for the first thirty minutes of it, saw much of the same with Teddy Jenks scoring his first goal for the club to put us three up, and although we conceded two late goals we managed to hold out for the win and celebrate for once.

Oh, and I almost forgot, new signing Ben Gladwin, came on in the second half and impressed with his stature and his touch. Roll on Gillingham away.

8th February 2023

The window has closed and time will tell if our dealings will come to fruition and we can escape relegation back to the 5th tier of English football. I would like to welcome our new players to Crawley Town, and hope that they all settle in quickly and provide the impetus to get us away from the trapdoor. Before I talk about Saturday's disappointing result, I would like to comment on the CTSA AGM that took place last Thursday. Unusually, we had a fairly good turnout and after the official business of the AGM had been conducted a frank and forthright discussion was held about the state of our club. It would only be fair to say that the feeling about our owners has somewhat diminished since they took over, but it would also be right to state that the situation is not beyond repair. One of our members expressed that the feeling was not anti-American, and gave as examples Wrexham and Gillingham. Whether it is 100% correct or not, he stated that Ryan Reynolds openly said he knew nothing about football and was happy "just" to provide the funds for the club to be run by people who know how to do it, whereas another member said. that at Gillingham, the owners would use the football club staff as sounding boards for their suggestions so as not to go off in the wrong direction.

Our owner, or rather the person who we perceive as being the "main man", whilst being a seemingly open and honest person, needs to learn how to take advice from those who know the realities of League 2 football and also how to learn from mistakes made. Vialli said you only learn from defeats and if you don't, then you will suffer even more of them. Now is the time to listen and learn.

Onto the game at Gillingham which we lost one nil. The away support was superb in number, but there are a few things that I would like to pick up on. It was inevitable that there would be some sort of Anti-Wagmi sentiment displayed, along with appreciative recognition of two players who had dome so much for Crawley Town. However, my opinion is that this should have been confined to before and after the match. The reason being that we were there to support our team, who must have thought at times that this was not the case. To hear "Super Tommy Nichols" being sung whilst the game was being played must surely have had Dom Telford thinking what's the point. I know that I will be pilloried for these thoughts, but hey, that's the way I have been brought up. I will not stand up when people sing "Stand Up" chants, mainly because I can't, but if you don't know I love Crawley Town, then that's your problem and not mine. I certainly do not like using the word "hate" as it is such an emotive word. Sunday morning, Dan Walker was on the tele, saying that his faith directs everything he does and says and I must admit I am the same, although it's not always easy.

Almost forgot, we lost one nil, that happens. Bring on Crewe

15th February 2023

I'm not going to talk about Stockport County or Orient away in this week's article as I was reminded in church this morning "do not worry about tomorrow, for tomorrow will worry about itself. Each day has enough trouble of its own." (Matthew 6:34)

That's for Tuesday and next Saturday, so let's talk about the game against Crewe Alexandra, shall we? In my opinion, once again, we did enough to win the game but almost came away with nothing because, once again in my opinion, we still lack the tall centre forward which will unlock the route to goal for Dom Telford. The window may be shut but there are still experienced big centre forwards available as free agents. I know this doesn't fit in with the Wagmi philosophy of getting young players, but I fear that without a player of that nature we might struggle to stay up. Caleb Chukwuemeka, is a big lad, and might still come good, but does he have enough experience? I understand he is carrying a slight injury at the moment so it might be worth looking for a replacement, even if it's only until the end of the season.

The game on Saturday saw us take the game to the opposition, with width being provided by Nick Tsaroulla on the left and

Kellan Gordon on the right. I lost count of the number of crosses that were provided, all of a reasonable height and pace for our two-prong attack of Telford and Nadesan, but it was a Crewe defender, Luke Offord, who put the final touch to a Gordon cross which broke the deadlock for Town, deflecting the ball into his own net.

As I walked round the pitch at half time, to hold February's Rollover draw, several people expressed my fear that we might rue the missed chances which fell to Dom Telford and Ashley Nadesan after we had taken the lead and, for an agonising thirty-seven minutes in the second half, it certainly looked that way as Crewe equalised on 50 minutes and took the lead on 60 from the penalty spot, when Kellan Gordon was, rather harshly, adjudged to have committed a foul in the box.

From that moment on Crewe did their utmost to slow the play down by feigning injuries, but in the end, they paid the price for their tactics when Ben Gladwin struck his first goal for the Reds in the 7th minute of injury time to earn the Red Devils a justifiable share of the spoils.

One thing that I hope Preston Johnson, Chris Galley and most importantly Scott Lindsey do this week, is look at the centre forward issue, as bringing Joel Lynch on to play up front certainly seems to say that is what is needed.

Perhaps worth having a look at the likes of Connor Wickham, Lewis Grabban and Leon Clarke. The last two having connections with Crawley, Lewis through his dad Gary, and Leon as an ex-Red himself. Both probably not the age to suggest a long career in Sussex, but worth a gamble if they keep us up.

I will leave you with an optimistic slant on the goal from Ben Gladwin that claimed the point on Saturday. "We might look back at the end of the season and say that was the goal that kept us up" credit Steve Herbert

22nd February 2023

I don't like quoting Liverpool managers, as wasn't it Bill Shankly who said 'Some people believe football is a matter of life and death, I am very disappointed with that attitude. I can assure you it is much, much more important than that. ' Clearly a crass statement to make, ask anyone who has lost someone, especially in tragic circumstances. However, when I watched Match of the Day on Sunday morning, I heard the present Liverpool boss say this; "When you are not in your best moment, you have to be ready to fight ".

Quite clearly, our club, Crawley Town, are not in "their best moment" as at 5pm on Saturday 18th February, thus it is now time for all who love the club to continue the fight until the season is over. With over 400 Red Devils present at Brisbane Road, the support could not be faulted, well, certainly not in quantity. As everyone knows, we lost by one goal to a team who are running away with League two. True, we could have lost by four or even more, but as I witnessed on Match of the Day, we could have also sneaked a totally unjustifiable one all draw. If only we had a forward like Nottingham Forest had.

So where do we go from here? We must remain positive, as, at the beginning of last week, most people were predicting worse defeats than we experienced. Stockport fans were complimenting us on our play, and, whilst we didn't play particularly well at Orient, we only lost by one goal.

The support, in terms of numbers, was exceptional, both at Stockport and in London. However, whilst expecting some anti Wagmi sentiment before and after the Orient game, I was disappointed to hear it during a game, which would have been hard enough for the players because of who we were playing. Had the chants not included slanderous comments about one of our owning consortia and truly horrible and crude comments about another, I could have possibly accepted the Wagmi Out chants but when the game drew to its expected conclusion and some fans, of all ages, started to sing to the players about them not being fit to wear the shirt, I could only turn and challenge those who thought it appropriate. The players who the chants were aimed at are what we must rely on to get us away from the relegation places, albeit with the addition of Tsaroulla, Gladwin, Jenks and others, so surely it is better to encourage them rather than berate them.

Preston Johnson and Scott Lindsey both stated that we didn't play as well as we could have, and it was clear in Scott's after match talk that he was as gutted as any stalwart fan at the performance. The noticeable part of his talk, for me, was there was no mention of the travelling support, and who could blame either the interviewer or him for that, after the abuse he received at the final whistle from a small minority of our "fans".

A difficult week has passed with respect to two away fixtures against two top seven clubs, and indeed it doesn't get much easier with 3rd placed Carlisle making the long journey south on Saturday.

May your support do what it says on the tin and may any criticism be positive.

1st March 2023

Going into the game against Carlisle United, Crawley Town sat in 23rd position and in the relegation places. However, our position was helped last Tuesday by both Hartlepool and Rochdale succumbing to defeats. They have both played four more games than the Red Devils and sat just one point ahead and five points adrift respectively. We were also at least ten goals better off in terms of goal difference than both of them.

Simple equation then. Do what they do or better when we are all playing and win the games that we have in hand. The games in hand are away to Tranmere and Sutton and home to Doncaster and Grimsby. An improvement in away results would do us no harm at all and a return to the Fortress Broadfield mentality would also be advantageous.

Coming out of the five two defeat to Carlisle the only statistic that remains the same is the number of games in hand we have over Hartlepool and Rochdale, albeit that our goal difference has worsened by three goals and they both earned draws coming from behind to achieve them.

The first of our games in hand will have taken place by the time you read this (sounding like an old man) in black and white on paper, and one can only hope that we won't have wasted the opportunity it gives us. Tranmere sit in 13th whilst our next two games are away to 4th placed Northampton and 9th placed Sutton. No doubt there will be some amongst us who can see no way out of our current position but three points from any of these games, or indeed all of them, must be what we aim for.

I share the fears that we will still be on 26 points by the time we see each other again for the first of our £2 games against Harrogate, but I hope we will be on 35 or somewhere in-between 26 and 35. The initiative, by the football club, to get people into the Broadfield for the games against fellow strugglers, Harrogate and Rochdale, has to be applauded as it is surely that only as "Town, Team, Together" that we stand a chance of getting out of our current predicament and maintaining our Football League status.

I will be watching Tuesday and Saturday on Ifollow in my own fan zone, which brings me to pointing out how sad it was that the opening of the Club's fan zone coincided with such a shattering loss. The atmosphere in the zone would have been electric if the score had been reversed.

In closing, I would like to thank everyone who contributed to Saturday's bucket collection for Parkinson's UK. Tongue in cheek, this could be the last collection for PUK at the Broadfield, as it seems to affect our results, with us losing on the last three occasions when it has taken place. Four-one to Port Vale, two-nil to Orient and five-two to Carlisle.

Speaking as a Parkinson's sufferer, I would like to point out that it was Parkie shaking my bucket, and not me!!

8th March 2023

Today is the first day of the rest of my life, or so sang John Denver way back in 1969. That was the year we were promoted to the 5th tier of English football, the Southern League Premier Division, as it was then. Why am I rambling on about John Denver and past glories, I hear you say? Because we as a club must treat the next game as the first day of the rest of the season if we are to get out of the predicament, we are currently in.

Hopefully, we will have started the rest of the season by bringing home some points from Gander Green Lane, but if we didn't, by the time you read this we must maintain that stance until the mathematics is either for us or against us.

Certainly, a big crowd and a bit of luck, as regards certain players being declared fit, could go a long way to us gaining a win at the Broadfield, next Saturday against Harrogate. We, the supporters, must get behind the team from the first minute until the last and hope that the players respond with an emphatic victory.

A victory would be made easier if we had someone prepared to shoot or set up the ammunition for those who are. In twenty games this season, just one more goal in each of them would have yielded us another twenty-eight points and we would be sitting on fifty-four points and be in the play-off positions. You could argue that if we had conceded one less goal in each of our matches we would also be in a much-improved position, but I would prefer us to be scoring more than just 1.06 goals per game, wouldn't you?

Our letting go of forward players, who not only score goals but create them as well, without replacing them is a mistake that people must learn from, whatever league we are in next season. To let them go is one thing, but to let them go to a relegation rival is something that I still cannot understand, no matter how many times it is explained to me. Perhaps bringing back out on loan forwards might also have helped.

What's needed? One more goal than the opposition in every game would be wonderful, but not realistic. Draws in every game would see us finish on forty points, which maybe enough, but winning seven of them, even if we lost the others, would gain us twenty-one points.

Still, it is what it is, and we, players, management, staff, supporters and, most importantly owners, must do our utmost in the next fourteen games to turn the season around.

It isn't over yet and wins in our three games in hand and the games against Harrogate, Hartlepool and Rochdale, could just about give us something to celebrate in May, almost as much as if we had won promotion.

15th March 2023

Where do I start? I didn't go to Sutton because of a knee injury, it's not only the players who get injured you know. I did watch it on Ifollow though, and at the end of the game felt, I would imagine, just like all other Crawley Town fans, totally depressed and fearing the worst. This was no doubt made worse by me updating my self-designed survival graph, showing us having lost our sixth game in a row, and being at least four wins below the survival line. Like the Duckworth-Lewis system used in cricket (not really) it shows what points total we should be on after the number of games we have played, in order to reach the magical 50 points after 46 games. After Sutton, thirty-three games played, we should have been on thirty-six points, but found ourselves on only twenty-six, ten points behind schedule.

Putting the depressing stuff aside for a few days, I got out my red tinted specs, watched "Making History" and "Back-to-Back" and started once more to believe. Whether or not my medication was affecting me, I don't know, but I dreamt the tensest finish to this season and came up with this scenario. We just need to win two games to stay up, if they are against Hartlepool and Rochdale and as long as they don't pick up any more points.

Not likely to happen, I know. We can definitely beat them but expecting them to lose their last eleven games is probably hoping too much. So, on Saturday I dug out my 80s scarf, crossed my fingers, prayed for divine intervention and set off for Broadfield Stadium. I knew we were in for a good day when I met my friend and his son on the number 10 bus. The last time we caught the same bus was on Boxing Day a few years back when we demolished the Cobblers by four goals to nil, winning my friend a large amount of money from his customary four nil home win bet.

Once again, he had placed his customary bet and at one stage it really looked like he might achieve another lucrative pay out, but unfortunately for him it wasn't to be. However, in front of over 3000 Red Devil fans the team showed what they can do with a totally committed display, from the kickoff to within five seconds of added time when Harrogate snatched an undeserved consolatory goal in a three one win for Crawley Town. What was the difference from Tuesday? Tilley was back, but Lynch was out suspended and Tsaroulla, Gladwin and Omole were still out injured, but the rest of the team chased, harried and generally produced the most consistent ninety minutes this season. Aramide Oteh scored two well worked goals and Jordan Mutch rounded off a fine display by scoring his first goal for the club in a polished performance.

We now sit just two and a half wins under the survival line and wouldn't it be great to break the away form record at Plough Lane next week. Looking forward to seeing you there.

22nd March 2023

What a wonderful weekend. Travelling up to Wimbledon was no problem, despite another strike by the RMT, and we were in the Wibbers Inn just after eleven. Train, tram, bus and Shansky's pony saw us to the pub, where we were soon joined by other Reds fans, all of whom were confident about getting a result, at Plough Lane, later in the day. The confidence ebbed just a little, when the teams were posted on twitter, as Kellan Gordon was missing through illness, but Joel Lynch and Ben Gladwin were on the bench. The other bit of news that stoked the fires was the rumour that AFC were going to parade Super Danni Bulman on the pitch before kickoff.

On the walk to the ground, I chatted to some Wimbledon supporters who clearly thought they were going to beat us, but you can never take anything for granted with Crawley Town, and so it proved. After going through airport style security to enter the ground, it was clear that the numbers of Crawley fans present had been affected by either the industrial action on the railways, the ridiculous cost of tickets to watch a League 2 encounter or the misreporting of the train strike.

Here's a tip, if you want to enter a ground quickly, carry a walking stick, and preferably one where the black paint has rubbed off leaving it looking like a blind person's aid. I am only joking, of course.

The rumour about the Icon, that is Danni Bulman, was almost right, but he was in civilian dress and not wearing the colours of any of his clubs. He was received warmly by all in the stadium, but it was the Crawley fans who serenaded him in song with "One Danni Bulman, there's only one Danni Bulman".

From the start of the game, it was obvious that the Crawley coaching team had managed to get the Reds in the right frame of mind for the battle. Before Ashley Nadesan blasted a James Tilley cross into the back of the Wimbledon net on six minutes, he had already been put through on goal, only to hit his shot over the bar. There were a few tense moments at the back for the Reds, but generally the defence played well, which was borne out by Wimbledon not having a single shot on target and only gaining one corner kick.

The only downside of the game was injuries to both Jordan Mutch and Ludwig Francilette, but their replacements, Ben Gladwin and Joel Lynch, proved to be more than adequate substitutions and saw us through to a famous win which was greeted with rapturous applause from the fans in The Cherry Red Records stand.

The trip home, with police escort, proved a little more difficult and thanks must be given to Rees Hopcraft for not giving up on this geriatric fan.

So, survival chart filled in and three home games on the trot to come, we could be on the survival line by ten pm on Tuesday 28th of March. Only Doncaster, Rochdale and Grimsby stand in our way and then it is up to us to maintain that form to the end of the season.

29th March 2023

Just after our one all draw with Doncaster Rovers, I started to go down with a sore throat. It could have been down to the excessive amount of chanting, shouting or singing (call it what you like) which accompanies watching any football team, but as the week wore on it became obvious that it was a medical problem that was causing it. So, on Saturday I took the responsible decision to have a Covid test which indicated that I was not suffering from that malady. The only time I've felt positive about being negative.

Knowing that I was probably only suffering from Influenza Homo Sapiens, I took myself down to Broadfield Stadium to watch the first of our must-win games against Rochdale. Rochdale sat seven points below us at kick off time, and really should have been a goal down within ten seconds of kick off, when Ashley Nadesan was sent clear only to see his shot deflected past the far post. The game then settled into a really open encounter which had the 4700 crowd on edge with both teams having chances to open the scoring.

From my unusual viewing position of the halfway line in the East stand, unusual for me that is, I witnessed new fans, infrequent fans and long-term fans joining together to cheer the Red Devils on, and, indeed, go into absolute ecstasy as Dom Telford and Dion Conroy put Crawley two up going into the break. At half time I debated with friends that we should really be four goals to the good, with the attempt at ten seconds and an even unluckier attempt from Nadders which came back off the far post with the keeper well beaten.

Moan time now. Half time was spoilt, a little, by two bits of behaviour, which were not meant to annoy but made it difficult to get around the stadium. The walkways are just that and are not the place to stand and chat and Stewards should be advising people of this, instead of just looking at people. A minor point I know, but one that would make everyone's matchday experience better.

Reverting to my usual standing position in Torres corner, alongside my family, we witnessed the team fully deserve the final time result of two nil and the use of substitutions that did not weaken the team but allowed some of our players much needed rest and/or game time.

Where does this leave us? Not, as some of our young fans were chanting at half time, "Staying up". Not quite, not yet. I am absolutely positive we will, but it must be mathematically proven before we start to celebrate in earnest.

Tuesday (last night) we face Grimsby in our last game in hand over Hartlepool and Rochdale, and God willing if our players perform as they can, there is absolutely no reason why we shouldn't be at least five points and eleven points clear of them respectively by ten o'clock on the 28th of March. That would leave us in the driving seat, but, as we all know, accidents can happen.

5th April 2023

Finding this hard, the day after a heavy defeat and Hartlepool and Rochdale both winning. But hey ho, it's gone now, and we must prepare for Good Friday and another crunch match with Bradford City. That's all of us, management, players and supporters alike.

Having just listened to Scott Lindsey's interview, not accompanied by a player this time, it is obvious that he is hurting from the display at Mansfield and openly admits the defending was poor but also stated that the attackers lacked confidence and were shy in taking their chances.

This reminds me of Mr. Jepson, my old PE teacher at Hazelwick, who, when asking the following question, put something into my brain which has just reemerged after fifty-nine years.

"Who in your team is responsible for defending and attacking?" Being reticent preteenagers, nobody wanted to answer until one brave soul put up his hand and announced, "It's obvious Sir, defenders defend, attackers attack". If we had been on QI the klaxon would have sounded and minus points won, or should that be lost?

Mr. Jepson, the teacher who taught me how to swim by throwing me into the pool, explained his philosophy. All eleven players on the pitch are responsible for both at all times whilst they are on the pitch. If they don't accept that responsibility, then they shouldn't cross the white line.

Obvious really, isn't it? The more time you spend in the opposition's half, the more likely it is that you will be successful in both attacking and defending. This requires concentration and commitment on everybody's behalf, as attack can very quickly turn into having to defend, and that is where the next adage comes in. "If you don't shoot (or head) you won't score" is where attackers start the defense in the next phase of the game. Likewise, defenders, including goalkeepers, can start attacks and must not be shy of getting the ball forward. This can be, as in the old BBC quiz, Quizball, either using the midfield (route four) or by bypassing them using a more direct approach, (route one). Routes two and three involve the midfield, but in a more direct or less shilly shallying manner. They can all work, Balcombe to Telford at Turf Moor or Mazeed's first Crawley goal at Mansfield are examples.

Scott Lindsey must now rebuild the confidence before next Friday, as Mark Hughes' Bradford are still hunting a play-off place, but even if we lose, a good battling performance is a must if we are to finish the season confidently. What can we, the supporters, do to assist them in this task? Well, the answer is in the name. We must support, from the first minute to the very last, in a positive and encouraging manner. Leave the negative stuff till after the game as I am sure this does not make the players perform any better.

Seven games left, two and eight points above Hartlepool and Rochdale respectively, and one point behind Colchester. We must, I feel, beat Colchester and Hartlepool and three of our remaining games, which will leave the monkey hangers requiring to win all their remaining games to send us down.

Simples!!!!!

12th April 2023, Fans Panel

Happy Anniversary, or is it? April 7th, 2022, Wagmi take over Crawley Town Football Club and who could have foreseen the rollercoaster of a ride through their first year. I know some of you will be thinking it has been more like riding on Oblivion at Alton Towers, with one huge down and not a lot of ups, but let's have a look at what has or has not been achieved.

On the playing side we have had some success in the Carabao cup, notching up our third Premier League scalp by beating Fulham, and putting on a creditable performance away to Premier League bound Burnley. We have got through three managers before arriving at the Scott Lindsey era and have failed to get any higher than 18th in the league. Currently, we sit in 22nd, fighting for our Football League lives. Added to that, the failure in all other cup competitions seems to paint a totally black picture of Wagmi's first year.

However, football, like any other way of life, is a one-off journey that can't be re-run. You can only move forward. Hartlepool and Rochdale are not run by Wagmi, but are still below us in the league, and we might have been even lower under different owners. Don't get me wrong, I am not happy with where we are, and I do feel that failure to listen to advice given, or listen but not take it into account, has contributed to where we find ourselves today.

Good things have been done, the fan zone and trying to engage fans are big pluses, and I know from first-hand knowledge that Preston Johnson has also supported local initiatives away from the club. However, here is my plea to WAGMI, focus on listening to people who know the game here in England, and then act on their advice, whatever League we find ourselves in come May 8th.

12th April 2023

Part one

In a game that threatened to ignite the embers of the Battle of Bradford in 2011, Crawley Town thoroughly deserved their share of the points from a pulsating encounter that saw both teams wanting three points but having to settle for just one. On a normal day the 2800 Crawley fans would, I believe, have gone home satisfied with the effort shown and the point gained, however, results elsewhere tempered the feeling somewhat, as Hartlepool and Rochdale both scored four time and collected three points each whilst Colchester and Harrogate both got a point apiece. These results are even more remarkable in that the monkey hangers only had five shots, of which four were goals, and Harrogate scored twice in the last minute to snatch a draw against the plastics. Eight points now cover the bottom five teams, Harrogate on forty, Colchester thirty-nine, Crawley and Hartlepool on thirty-eight and Rochdale on 32. I am not downhearted just yet, as I really feel that we will beat a team by more than one goal before the end of the season, and hopefully it will be against Colchester at home and Hartlepool away. Before the Barrow game our goal difference advantage that we had over the two teams below us has virtually dissipated, whilst we are nine goals behind Colchester and Harrogate. The gap between us and the Essex side could disappear with a five-nil home win against them on the 18th, but it would also help us if Stevenage ,

Mansfield and Crewe could pull off victories Easter Monday, whilst we attempt to do the same up in Cumbria.

Part two

Well, there I was ready for Barrow and prepared to give the benefit of the doubt to Scott Lindsey's team selection, unlike some Crawley supporters, thinking that Telford, Tilley, Oteh and Gordon must be carrying injuries if not included in the starting lineup, and judging by the performance given by the team that surely must have been the case. Even when the first three came on towards the end of the first half and at the beginning of the second, we looked like a team that didn't think we could get a result and that proved to be correct. The minute you let your shoulders drop you have lost the game in my opinion and we got what we deserved out of the game. Nothing.

What did the others down the bottom do? They all gained points against better teams, Colchester winning four nil and Harrogate, Hartlepool and Rochdale showing real fight to gain draws against Leyton Orient, Stevenage and Mansfield respectively. Our goal difference advantage has now been wiped out and we lie five points ahead of Rochdale and one behind 'Pool.

Saturday against Tranmere is now enormous and hopefully we will be able to select our best team. Not much to ask, is it? Come on Newport, Bradford and Salford, help us out.

19th April 2023

I could write about all the remaining games of each of the bottom eight teams, but what would be the point? We, Crawley Town FC, now know that if we match the results, or better them, of the two teams below us we will be in League 2 next season. Our destiny is back in our own hands, or should that be feet, once again.

Following on from the defeat at Barrow a win was a must against Tranmere and certainly, with the inclusion of Gladwin, Gordon,

Conroy and Tsaroulla in the first eleven, the level of optimism amongst the Reds faithful had risen in Redz pre-match.

Crawley, being Crawley, then set about redeeming themselves for the display in Cumbria only for Corey Addai to bring us all down to earth again with his unfortunate slip which let in Tranmere's Saunders for the first goal of the game. What was the reaction? From the players it was positive with some good football being played throughout the team. From Supporters it was more than that as the players rested last week, ran themselves almost into the ground, seeking a way to create a season's first, a win from a losing position.

After 30 minutes the breakthrough came, when Aramide Oteh put a defender on his back side before slamming the ball past Hewelt in the Rovers' goal. A sublime goal, which was followed just ten minutes later when Jack Powell got his backside to a Harry Ransom header to send the Reds in two one up at half time. The goal was reminiscent of Dannie Bulman's first professional goal for Wycombe Wanderers and for many scored by a Town Mead Wanderers centre forward, back in the early seventies. The name has been omitted to save him his blushes but suffice it to say he still supports the mighty Reds.

During half time the scores from other games were coming in and raising the optimism levels back to pre-match levels and the players responded by giving their all, not just to hold on, but to try and increase their lead. Then, with just eight minutes left, our whole world threatened to cave in around us. Mazeed, on for Nick Tsaroulla, was harshly judged to have handled a Sam Taylor low cross and a penalty was awarded.

Kane Hemmings hit his penalty to Corey's right and the big shot stopper dived full length to parry the effort into the path of Rhys Hughes, who then blasted the ball past the far post. The crowd went wild, the outfield players celebrated with the keeper and after seven additional minutes over and above the ninety we, players, supporters, management and yes, owners, celebrated in earnest as Black-Eyed Peas played over the loudspeakers. Redemption earned.

I mention the owners, as I am sure Preston Johnson would have celebrated as much as anyone, despite having to watch the game in the safety of his London hotel because of threats of violence made against him. Mistakes have been made and need to be put right before we, hopefully, kick off in League Two for the 2023/2024 season.

Remember, football is one of the most important of the least important things in life.

26th April 2023

Where to start? That is the question. Writing this on St George's day after having just got an hour ago, after, what was, one of those days which will go down in Crawley Town history.

90 minutes of football, only to have to travel those 300 miles back in the same day, may seem a bit silly to some but, looking back the day after, it must be said it was well worth it.

Some will not remember it as well as others, no names no pack drill, but for me the two-nil victory will go down, alongside Welling, Tamworth, Accrington and Hull City away as one of the most significant in our history.

I know we are not mathematically safe yet, as there are still six points that Hartlepool can win, and we can throw away. We currently have a six-goal difference advantage over Jeff Stelling's team, which could disappear with two wins for them and two losses for us. This, however, is not going to happen as Scott Lindsay now has a whole week to prepare the team for our home game against Walsall and I am positive that we will be well over the finish line by 5pm next Saturday.

Back to the game, it was good to see that the Football League Paper honoured two of our players with places in their League Two Team of the Week. They are of course Dom Telford, who comes into some criticism from some of our fans because he hasn't scored as many goals for us as he did for Newport County, although he is still our leading scorer, and Corey Addai because he isn't Glenn Morris. Well, all I can add to that is Dom scored a brace yesterday, one with his head and the other with a sublime piece of skill, and Corey made several saves yesterday, claimed everything in the air and made the pass of the day to set up Telford for the crucial second goal. Surely, the world record for the longest assist!!

The train journey home was one of celebration which, I hope, was enjoyed by Dion Conroy, his mum and dad and Anthony Grant, who travelled back to London with us, but also one of serious discussion of where we go from here, and of explaining the intricacies of goal difference to those who needed it and the need to double check information given to you in a pub by an opposing supporter of the opposite sex.

Sir Carl Aarvold, Alice Bendle, Brian Clough, H'angus the Monkey, Janick Gers, Private Theo Jones. John Askey.

We have beaten them all, we have beaten them all

Jeff Stelling, can you hear me? Jeff Stelling, your boys took one hell of a beating! Your boys took a hell of a beating!!!

Now let's make sure we don't let this opportunity pass us by. Not just the opportunity to stay in the Football League, but also, with a little bit of luck, to finish above AFC Wombles.

3rd May 2023

Over 4000 people were in the ground at our last home game hoping for the right result to maintain our Football League status. Whilst we didn't win, we gained the point that was to relegate Hartlepool, despite them beating Barrow by three goals to one. As I stood applauding the efforts of Scott Lindsey and his team, I looked around the stadium at our support and, with a bit of a tear in my eye, thought how good it was to see so many celebrating our survival in front of Preston Johnson. If he was in any doubt as to what the club means to the fans, that must surely have been dispelled on Saturday. Just imagine what the atmosphere was like at Hartlepool, as they awaited the end of our game.

What next? Wagmi out or Wagmi in? What is needed is an admittance of mistakes made, lessons learnt and an apology for what has been a season of ups and, mostly, downs. My point of view is that this is imperative if the relationship between the fans and the owners can be restored. Counting Preston Johnson as a friend, I know that he has been affected by the season in ways he could not have foreseen before he thought of buying an English football club and that he wants to stay and put things right. However, this is not a one-way street. We, the fans, must now weigh up whether we can give him the chance to put things right. Once again, in my opinion, I think we should. We should also keep up a meaningful dialogue with them regarding the general running of the club and be prepared to acknowledge mistakes made by all connected with the club, whether they be committed by Owners, Staff, Players and, yes, even by us, the fans.

We should also be prepared to acknowledge the positive efforts made by all connected with the club and how they are linked with each other. The increase in our attendances at home, up by over 35%, and the fantastic increase in those who are prepared to travel to way games, either by coach, car or train must be applauded, but the question must be asked, what has led to this happening? Usually, when a team goes down the league, gates fall. We have bucked the trend. Why?

We now, weather permitting, train on grass, which fans were asking for under the previous regime. We have a fans zone to improve the match day experience, something which has long been needed.

But we have also had four managers in one season, numerous communication bloopers and inappropriate responses to all that has happened since the beginning of the season.

Anyway, we are still a Football League side, and I for one will be up for a party on the 8th of May in Swindon regardless of the result. From watching the last two games I have noticed that there are players playing who probably shouldn't and who are in

238

desperate need of a rest and the end of the season. The fact they have done so well in the last four games shows their commitment to the cause, which is Crawley Town FC. 2023/2024 our 13th Football League season beckons.

10th May 2023

Before we faced Swindon Town on Bank holiday Monday I decided to look at some statistics for 2022/2023 just for a bit of fun and to see where our weaknesses were in what proved to be an exciting season for all the wrong reasons, but before I do, I would like to thank all those who properly read last week's article and to stress to everyone that I don't get paid by anyone for my thoughts.

Anyway, I thought I would look first at the games where we lost by a single goal or drew, and what effect scoring one more goal in each of those games would have meant. Amazingly, it would have put us in second place with 84 points and promoted. Forget that for a moment and consider what would have happened if we had conceded one less goal in those same games without scoring anymore ourselves. Not quite as beneficial, but we would still have accrued 74 points, which would have seen us just below the play off positions going into the Swindon game. However, if we had scored more and conceded less in those games, we would have finished with 111 points and be champions. Which only goes to show that you can do anything with statistics. Our goals for, before the Swindon game, stand at just one a game, whereas our goals against stand at one and a half. Which is exactly why we are where we are. However, what the stats do show, I believe, is that we are more in need of someone up front than we need more defenders.

And then I went to Swindon and was absolutely blown away by the quantity and volume of our support, which lasted throughout the whole 98 minutes of play and beyond, as grateful supporters gave their thanks for a sterling effort which unfortunately yielded no points reward, as once again, we were defeated by the odd goal in three. I am only going to report on positive matters today and I include here two quotes from the Swindon Advertiser shortly after the game.

"Crawley were playing the more cohesive **football** in the first half," and "With five minutes to play, Crawley cut through Swindon like a hot knife through butter down the left and almost forged a wonderfully-worked equalizer. Ashley Nadesan's left-footed cross was met by Tom Fellows about six yards out, but Brynn spread himself really well to deny the defender."

Ok, I missed out the two goals in four minutes just before half time, but I must add they were not a true reflection of the play, and when Dom Telford stroked home a penalty, awarded for a foul on Nick "He must stay" Tsaroulla, Crawley looked like they might just get a result. However, just before the "almost forged a wonderfully worked equalizer" move Swindon were awarded a penalty of their own, only to see Corey Addai make his second penalty save in a row.

A thoroughly entertaining game which, in my opinion, gives us hope for 2023/2024. When do the fixtures come out?

17th May 2023

The first Saturday of the close season and I feel lost already. I am watching Leeds United V Newcastle United as I write this, but it's not real football to me without the personal connection. Having said that, I do understand how the supporters at Elland Road must be feeling. Anyway, let's get back to Crawley Town and where we go from here.

Firstly, I wouldn't have a mass clear out of players as, in my opinion, we just need some thoughtful pruning and grafting to change our team into one that will bring more smiles next season. I would offer Harry, Ludwig and Nick Tsaroulla extensions to their contracts, as all three are young and will only get better. The loan players will be back with their parent clubs after a short break, but I would like Tom Fellows and Mazeed to be looked at again for next year as I feel there is something about them that deserves another taste of all action League Two men's football. Where we strengthen is, or should be, down to Scott and Jamie to ponder, but for a start I think most fans would be happy with strengthening in goal, defence, midfield and attack with quality being more important than quantity.

Off the field, all interested parties need to look at what is best for our club as we seek to rise from the nadir of the season just gone. Wagmi and the CTSA need to communicate with each other in a positive and constructive manner and feed their agreed decisions to the entire fan base in a timely manner. Patience is a virtue, or so it is said, but football supporters very rarely show that quality. Now the season is over the fans are keen to know what will be different next season, and I believe by the time you read this Wagmi will have issued an initial statement as regards the status of our club. It won't answer all the questions raised but will, I hope, at least give a timeline of where we go from here and what we need to do to achieve some measure of success.

What will our division look like next season? Will it be more Northern and will we have more miles to travel?

Well, we have lost Hartlepool, Rochdale, Orient, Stevenage and Northampton before the League Two play offs have kicked off, and have gained Wrexham, Milton Keynes, Accrington Stanley, Morecambe, Notts County and Forest Green Rovers. Meanwhile, the first semifinals of the League Two playoffs have taken place, with home sides Salford City and Bradford City both gaining one nil advantages against Stockport County and Carlisle United respectively. All northern sides, with Carlisle being my desired choice, to gain the last promotion spot, for two very good reasons. The number of miles it is from north Sussex to Cumbria and because we, Crawley Town, managed to take points off the other three sides.

Let's hope for some relatively speedy news re ticket prices, retained list and new players etc. and for the bad memories of last season to fade quickly away.

24th May 2023

Before I start on the retained and released list it is good to see that Carlisle are doing their best to rid us of our longest away trip. Surely Bradford City are too big a club to be in League 2 with us upstarts. A club with their history, founded in 1903, as opposed to us founded in 1896. A club with superior support, 4% of their city's population against our paltry 2.5%. A club who were not promoted into the Football League but were elected in their first year of existence, as opposed to us who, at the time, gained promotion with a record points total. You simply cannot compare us, except on the field where it shows the upstart crows having won seven out of fourteen games played and having lost only four. Indeed, the record against them is even better if you just count League Two results, six wins, three draws and just one defeat. Salford City will also give us the opportunity to earn more points against them, with us only losing once in eight games played and having a 100% home record against them. Seriously, good luck to Carlisle and Stockport County in next week's final.

My son and I spoke to Preston Johnson last Friday and asked him questions which he understood were right and proper to be asked and explained the reasons and the background that culminated in us having to fight against relegation during 2022/23, all of which will no doubt will be shared with the fans when appropriate. The first sign of them communicating with the fan base for the coming season is the publishing of the retained and released list, although I do accept there are probably more questions to be answered from the publication.

Players under contract

Will Craig and Hessenthaler, be allowed to prove their loyalty to Crawley Town or be loaned out or sold in the transfer window?

Joel Lynch, when fit an invaluable player for Crawley Town, can he remain fit longer this season?

Florian Kastrati and Jed Brown, presumably will be given a chance in pre-season to prove their worth to Crawley Town.

Will Kwesi Appiah, be allowed to prove both his fitness and goal scoring abilities in pre-season.?

Players remaining in contract talks with the club:

Rafiq Khaleel and Aramide Oteh, in my opinion, should be persuaded to stay for at least another year as both proved valuable in the fight against relegation

Roshan Greensall falls into an area where we don't know enough about him to gauge whether he is up to keeping goal in League 2, and I do feel that we are in need of a keeper who can challenge for the first team spot, with no disrespect intended to Corey Addai.

Players having had one-year extensions taken up by the club

Nick Tsaroulla and Harry Ransom, nothing to say here but well done to all involved.

Players released or going back to their parent clubs

The only two that I am upset about are Tom Fellows and Ludwig Francilette, and I would like Tom to return on loan and for Ludwig perhaps to be granted another chance.

All a matter of opinion, I know. New players needed? What do you think?

31st May 2023

Well, that's it, the E F League 2 season is finally over with Carlisle United clinching the fourth promotion spot, defeating Stockport County in a penalty shoot-out, to cut our travelling costs just a little, as we prepare for what is looking increasingly like EFL 2 North. At least for one season anyway?

We can now chant that ubiquitous "dirty northern ********" chant at all of our games, if you feel so inclined. Personally, I would much rather hear positive, encouraging chants aimed at our players and maybe the officials. You know the sort, where you are imploring our players to shoot more often, tackle more enthusiastically, pass the ball forward etc etc and where you might be suggesting that next time the linesman might stand a better chance of giving offside if he, she or they were actually up with play.

I have just read through the over twenty questions that Mark Dunford collected from supporters to be asked of WAGMI, and I think they could all be answered by a fans' forum, but it has to be done sooner rather than later. I am sure, that in today's technological world, one could be even held over the magic of the internet before Preston Johnson or Eben Smith make the trip back to Crawley.

For me, having talked with Preston myself, I know he realises how much Crawley Town means to the Red Army. I hope he and Wagmi answer the questions soon, however they choose to do it, especially the ones re ticket prices, chief executive officer, director of football and improvements to the playing squad.

Having shouted "(Name of manager, chairman, owners) OUT "myself over my years of supporting Crawley Town, I do appreciate how the state of our club can affect people's emotions, mental health and finances. However, as I am now over the age of youthful excess, and having worked for the club back in 2011/12, I now understand, a little, what goes into running our club and that no one goes out to lose games or play badly on purpose, and that in any game of football there are three possible results. Win, Lose or Draw. Even that set of results can be expanded into; deserved it, daylight robbery, unlucky etc etc so I am going to say now, that perhaps we need to be more level headed in our support and more acceptable of any results that occur as long as our players, management and owners have given the proverbial 100% of effort into their actions, both on and off the pitch.

One of my favourite platitudes for when things aren't going right, used to be:

"Everything is going to be all right in the end. If it isn't, then it's not the end" courtesy The Best Exotic Marigold Hotel.

But now I've found an even better one:

"Everything is going to be all right. Or, if not, everything is going to be, so let's not worry"

I would be watching Crawley Town whatever league we were playing in, and I think that goes for many of the additional 30% of fans we have seen at home this season. How about you?

Stop Press

Max Watters comes on in extra time for Barnsley in League 1 but fails to save them against Sheffield Wednesday as, reduced to ten men since the 49th minute, they succumb to a goal in the third minute of extra time's additional time. Come home Max.

Part Four

Where do we go from here?

What a question and one that can only be answered with a determined frame of mind, whether that mind belongs to owners, manager, players or fans.

I am disappointed in that, as at the end of May 2023, there has been no thank you from the owners for the incredible support our "twelfth man" gave, especially towards the end of the season, which I believe made all the difference up at Hartlepool. This may be because of the vitriol poured out by, what I feel is, a minority of our supporters to the owners. I am of course not suggesting that anyone should be happy or complacent about last season, but some of the chanting has been infantile at best and disgusting at worst. We all have the right to shout "Sack the board" or similar comments but you should also consider what the alternative is. Have you got a multi-millionaire waiting in the wings or a consortium willing to put the sort of money in to run a successful League club, even at our level?

In talking to Preston, I have got the impression that he wants to build bridges and restore the faith of our fans in their "project" but I do feel this can only happen if all parties seek a conciliatory approach, with both sides willing to learn from mistakes made and make sure they don't happen again. I say both sides, but that infers there are only two opinions, whereas we all know there are probably as many as there are our supporters.

I hope the 30% rise in home attendances is maintained and that our squad is strengthened to face the future. Having just watched a Walsall fan rate the fans of all league two teams, giving us a grade of "tinpot", I felt hurt on everyone's behalf, but then, after some thought, I had to agree with him over one point he made. He was at the nil nil draw at the end of April 2023 and gave his verdict based on the number of our "supporters" wearing shirts of other clubs. I know you will say that's because of the lack of

246

supply of our own shirts, but that doesn't mean you have to wear a Tesco's carrier bag or the shirt of any other club you might like.

Anyway, having got that off my chest, let's make a date at the Broadfield, not just for next season, but for ever, or until we have to move to a bigger ground, whoever the owners may be.

NOLI CEDERE, TOWN TEAM TOGETHER

Milton Keynes UK
Ingram Content Group UK Ltd.
UKHW051345041223
433760UK00023B/447